NEVER AT
A LOSS FOR
AN OPINION

NEVER AT A LOSS FOR AN OPINION

PROFESSOR X

ARLINGTON HOUSE·PUBLISHERS
NEW ROCHELLE, N. Y.

Library of Congress Cataloging in Publication Data

Professor X., fl. 1973-
    Never at a loss for an opinion.

    1. College teaching as a profession. I. Title.
LB1778.P75   378.1'2'023   74-22132
ISBN 0-87000-280-5

For my Friends...

(The two I have left)

Contents

NEVER AT
A LOSS FOR
AN OPINION

Introduction

It was more than twenty years ago, but I still recall the incident vividly. A friend and I sat down to a Marine Corps breakfast, rubbing the sleep out of our eyes—and stared in disbelief at the mess that had been slopped on our trays. "You know," said my friend, "that cook has real talent." Seeing the look of astonishment on my face, he continued, "Well, an egg is hard to foul up. Your cook of just ordinary talent will mash and mangle an egg and it still comes out all right. But look at this stuff. I don't think it's edible. I tell you, it takes real talent to ruin an egg this way."

Similarly, some five years ago I met another man with real talent, a historian from a prestigious Southern university who was speaking at the annual Arts and Sciences dinner at our campus. His subject was American medical quackery, a topic you would swear no one could make dull; with all the nostrums and notions that have been peddled to a gullible public, with all the swindles perpetrated by confidence men selling salves guaranteed to make the old young and the young beautiful, this professor should have captivated and entertained his audience mightily. But he put them to sleep in short order, and that took real talent.

That night, sitting there, I first was embarrassed in the same way I am embarassed when I see a Jerry Lewis movie on television. If the fellow doesn't have enough sense to be embarrassed for himself, then I am embarrassed for him. Finally at this dinner, I began to feel like a student in the classroom once again; the same monumental boredom engulfed me that I had endured for so many years to become a professor. To entertain myself I let my mind wander over the proceedings of the evening. Suddenly I was struck by the concept of ritual suffering—the notion that after-dinner speaking in America is as stylized as a High Mass at a Catholic church. I jotted notes to myself on this: the sameness of the humor of that tired breed, the master of ceremonies; the introduction of honored guests at the head table; the introduction of the speaker for the evening, "a man who needs no introduction"; the ritual joke with which the speaker began his dry discourse; the ritual applause at the end of the speech; and the ritual line of people to congratulate the speaker afterward. And everyone there knowing all the while that the speech would be as bad as the student union food, if not worse—if that were possible.

The next day, nursing indigestion both of mind and stomach, I rewrote those notes into a four- or five-page essay which I put in the files. At the time I had no idea what I would do with it.

Months later I was teaching a seminar on the writing of history. One of the exercises in that class is a look at reviewing books and the writing of a review for publication. In previous years I had spoken more or less off the cuff about book reviewing and had tried to tell the students what I thought a good review should contain. This year, however, I decided to write out the lecture with total honesty on how the process worked, giving the insight I had gained working on a journal of history. That piece also went into the file with my thoughts about ritual suffering at after-dinner speeches.

Then came a visit by a "college representative," as traveling book salesmen for publishing houses are called, and I was moved to write out my thoughts on the selection of textbooks. Over the next several months I continued to draft my honest reaction to several aspects of the college profession. When these totaled about 40,000 words, I began thinking in terms of a book which would, in the jargon of students, "tell it like it is"—a totally honest and candid look at the world of professors. I took the twenty or so "chapters" I had written, pitched them into different piles until I thought I had some organization, and sent my manuscript off to Senior Editor David Franke at Arlington House. He replied that he was interested, but that the manuscript as it stood was too short. So I sat down, made up a list of additional subjects that would fit in one chapter or another, and wrote an additional 10,000 words. The result of all this was *This Beats Working for a Living: The Dark Secrets of a College Professor,* which Arlington House published late in March 1973.

I published the book anonymously as Professor X, figuring that if the book fell dead from the press I would be safe, for no one would ever hear of it. However, if the book proved successful, I still would be safe from great anger on the part of most of my colleagues because the one thing professors most admire is success; most of them have so little of it that they greatly admire it. And I thought that most of those who read it would never see themselves no matter how wretched they are at the business; rather, I thought they would say to themselves, "Yes, I know the guy he is talking about; it's that S.O.B. down the hall that I hate."

The book came out and I waited for a reaction. First came the reviews in newspapers. One of the reviewers who took a meat axe to me commented that apparently I started out to write a humorous, satirical book about the world of academicians but that apparently I began to take myself seriously about half way through the task; he concluded that the first half was good, the last half bad. I found that review interesting, even a typical analysis by a professor—for I had not written the book in the sequence in which it appeared in the book. (Here, as an aside, I note that some professors, especially those in English literature, can discern some of the most startling things from reading what an author has written. I recall one English professor who told me that he could tell the difference between something written originally in longhand and that first written on the typewriter. "The rhythm of the words is different," he informed me with that air of superiority so common to professors. Since that time I have lost some of my confidence in myself, for I have studied many books closely and have never been able to tell if the author wrote the original manuscript with a pencil or on the typewriter.)

Other newspaper reviewers, some journalists, some professors, had varied reactions. Some liked it, some hated it. Yet I had no quarrel with any of them so long as they read the book. Walter Prescott Webb, the great Texas historian, commented once, "Any man who can read is his own critic." Therefore I was content to let them say what they would—and waited to see what the local reaction would be. I had not really tried to disguise my identity too greatly, and anyone who knew me at all would, if he read the book, know I was the perpetrator.

About a week later a sales representative for one of the New York publishers came into my office and confronted me. I admitted the authorship and asked his opinion. "Oh, that's exactly what book salesmen say about professors when they get off the campus," he told me.

Then I began to get reactions from my fellow professors. One, a very competent man, told me, "I'm damned glad you wrote it—and damned glad I didn't," Well, so much for courage.

The first strong rumble of discontent with the book came from some Home Economics people. They found my thoughts about their discipline not to their liking (I had suggested that the field be abolished). Then, just as I was about to leave to do some publicity on the book, three or four individuals approached the president of the university to suggest that I should not be allowed to do any television shows or newspaper interviews. Naturally they suggested that this would be "for the good of the university" because the legislature was in session and might cut our appropriation. Fortunately the president of the institution where I teach is a good man—one of the finest administrators I have ever served under—and he turned down this approach. I still wasn't too worried because the ringleader of this group was a professor of humanities, a type for which I have about as much respect as I do for poets. Later I was talking with a member of the legislature from down-state and asked him if the book had caused any negative comments down in the capital. "What book?" he responded. Well, so much for legislators. And professors of humanities.

Later I was in Detroit doing a television talk show where the host had a local professor to play antagonist to my position. That professor was as angry a man as I ever want to meet. Something or other I said must really have hit home; he even refused to shake hands with me when I was introduced to him. Then, on the air, he accused me, among other things, of being prejudiced against women. I go sort of tickled at the poor fellow, and when he made that charge I responded that I didn't hate women, that in fact some of my best friends were women, and that "I'm even married to one, and I'd be delighted if my son married one." The moment the show was over, he stomped off the set—and almost strangled himself on his microphone cord. Later he wrote the Human Rights Commission here in my home state, as well as to some federal watchdog agency that looks into prejudice, to charge me with discriminating against women. He wanted a piece of my scalp pretty bad.

To my great surprise, however, a majority of the professors who discussed the book with me approved of it wholeheartedly. Some even did so openly. One psychologist told me he was going to send copies to all his colleagues for Christmas, while a historian at a nearby university with which we have a great rivalry slipped copies with certain passages underlined into four of his fellow historians' mailboxes.

Perhaps the greatest compliment of all came from students. While a few of my colleagues were referring to me as a "Smiling Old Boy," only abbreviating it, students dropped by as word spread to say nice things about it. In fact, one of my undergraduates, who had returned to complete his bachelor's degree after

15

an absence of ten years, decided to write a "Student X" book to overcome the boredom of the classroom and to entertain himself (see *Professors and Other Inmates*). And in the past year I have had several graduate students say they feel they could write a Graduate Student X book. In fact, one couple, a man and wife both completing their doctoral work, said they were thinking about doing a book about their experiences. The wife said she could tell some particularly interesting stories about what some of the members of her committee suggested she would have to do if she expected to pass. I know the particular faculty member at the institution she named; curiously, he was one whom friends told me was particularly vocal in denouncing me and my Professor X book. I encouraged the two, even suggesting that if they wrote such a book together they might list the authorship as X^2.

However, the highlight of this experience was that I was able to review *This Beats Working for a Living* in a standard, scholarly academic journal. I have always wanted to have one of my books reviewed by someone who thoroughly understood what I was trying to do, whose thoughts were similar to my own, and who would laud me in print. In fact, I considered it highly fitting that I was able to review the book myself—and it was a favorable review—for this was a kind of postscript to the book, showing just how bankrupt the system of academic reviewing is. I heard from some people that this review, when it appeared in print, actually made some professors angrier than the book itself had, for it helped to prove that what I had written was true.

What I am trying to say in all this is that I thoroughly enjoyed writing *This Beats Working for a Living,* that I enjoyed the reaction to it by those who liked it as well as those who hated it, and that writing a review of one of my own books was the highpoint of my life. Therefore I am venturing out into the realm of print once more under the pseudonym of Professor X, not only in the hope of reviewing this one also but because I have yet more to say about this group known as professors.

When I confided to a colleague that I was doing this second volume, he asked with more than a little seriousness, "What are you going to do? Look through the catalog and see who all you missed insulting the first time around?"

Some people accused me, after the first effort appeared, of being too hard on professors, saying the percentage of good ones was higher than I had indicated. To this I respond by asking them how many really fine professors they had studied under during the four years it took them to complete a bachelor's degree. Almost to a person (note, please, those of you who considered me to be antifeminine, that I did not say "almost to a *man*") the reply was "five or six." I then pointed out to these persons that the typical student has to pass 126 to 128 semester hours of work on a bachelor's degree, or a total of some 42 courses; that allowing for some duplication of professors they still had to study under some 35 professors; and that 5/35ths came to about fourteen percent good ones by their own estimation. Yet in my book I had calculated the percentage of good ones at about one-fourth. In short, most of those accusing me of being too harsh in my judgment of the profession, when asked to recall their own professors, were much harder on the breed than I am.

In doing this second book I want it known that like Martin Luther I recant nothing, I retract nothing, I regret nothing in the first volume. It is not that I can "do no other," but rather that what I wrote is true. Now I know the old cliché that "the truth shall make you free." My daddy put it much better many years ago when he commented, "The truth just makes you enemies." I continue the same theme in this new effort for the same reason: I hope the poor ones, mainly organized into the American Association of University Professors, will see themselves and change. The profession must cleanse itself or else the public is going to become very angry with us. The country needs good universities and cannot afford to have an angry public tearing up the system.

Finally, I want to say a word to those of you who purchase a copy of this book and then lend it to friends. I have had several people point out to me that they lent out their copy of *This Beats Working for a Living* to colleagues; one fellow in my department here noted that his father's copy had been read by no less than eighteen people. Let me point out that this is downright un-American! If you who purchase this one, refuse to lend it, others will have to buy it. This enables lumberjacks and papermakers to find employment; it keeps the printers working; it allows the publisher to pay higher dividends to its stockholders; and it brings greater royalties to me (and I am a confirmed member of the keep-the-currency-circulating crowd). In short, forcing the cheapskates to buy is good for the American economic system in this time of economic uncertainty. Tell anyone who wants to borrow your copy to go buy his own.

I
Employment in the Seventies

THE CHANGING JOB MARKET

Beginning about 1969 the number of jobs in higher education began to diminish rapidly. By 1971 there were so few jobs available that serious discussions began among professors about the reasons and remedies for the situation. Everyone could agree that the period of rapid growth of colleges and universities had come to an end, but there were many answers advanced to explain why. The end of the unpopular draft law caused many who had been in school only to avoid a two-year stint in the service to leave, while others who would have been draft-dodgers no longer needed to come to college. And there was the leveling off, even the diminishing birth rate of some eighteen years back, which meant that there were no longer a growing number of high school graduates each spring. Moreover, there was the alarming (to university professors) growth of the junior college system, which siphoned off an increasing percentage of those who did begin their higher education.

All these reasons could be advanced safely, but few mentioned the growing number of eighteen-year-olds who found college a monumental bore and passed this word along to their younger brothers and sisters, as well as their cousins and friends. In addition, many youngsters were discovering that at a vocational-technical school, they could learn some trade in one year, two at most, which would bring them as much income as would a college degree—as well as the satisfaction of working with their hands at something practical.

Whatever the causes, colleges and universities no longer needed to hire professors in virtually every department to staff classrooms for the incoming horde of freshmen each fall. Suddenly the job, which some professors seemed to think they were doing some institution a favor by taking, became something to be thankful for having. No longer could members of the profession move about like medieval monks living off the alms of the land—only in our case it was the taxes of the land. Yet the remedies suggested to ease this situation were about as practical as the courses which most professors were teaching.

Some immediately suggested that every graduate school in the country should limit the number of graduate students admitted to begin training. Here they wanted to imitate some of the professions which limit their membership, so all can be employed, through the entrance examination; for example, the test for those aspiring to be certified public accountants had no set passing score, but rather varies the passing grade upward or downward each year according to how many new ones can be taken in without overcrowding the field and diminishing the income of all. In the case of universities, such a call fell on deaf ears. Everyone realized that every graduate school in the country would have to work together to enforce this, for if one cut down and the next did not then the institution still taking all comers would grow rapidly. No, this suggestion was impractical.

Therefore, some professors began demanding that only a few select universities be allowed to award the doctorate and that all institutions which recently had inaugurated doctoral work abolish this. Again this proved impractical—as well as foolish. The American Historical Association, for example, cannot enforce any ruling about which schools can award the Ph.D. in history, nor can any of the other national associations in whatever discipline. Rather, this is done by the regents of the many institutions and by the regional accrediting associations. And the desire to limit the number of institutions giving the doctorate is foolish, for those who would do so would limit this to the few big-name universities—when it is at some of the smaller and newer institutions where the faculty is still trying that some of the best training takes place.

The result of all this talk is that nothing has been done to limit the production of new professors. And at some institutions there have been decreases in enrollment so that some faculty members have had to be let go; this usually is done in a nice way—the professor's contract is not renewed, and at the end of the academic year he no longer has a job. Therefore everyone walks around talking about the current "hard times" in higher education—and trying desperately to hang on to a position. Some are even nervous enough to try *working* as a means of not being fired.

However, in the long-range view of higher education, these are not hard times. As one historian told me, "You think back about the way employment for professors has run, and you find that the current situation really is the normal one. Right after World War II, when the veterans returned and enrollments swelled, there was a boom market, and then there was another one from about 1963 or 1964 to the end of that decade. But hard times are the normal, not the exception." In thinking about the situation, I have concluded that he is right.

Yet it has taken several years for this information to sink into the minds of many professors. I suspect that more than half the academicians in the United States came into the job market within the past ten years, and all they knew for most of that period was the boom period. I still hear one of these unenlightened types, when angry, declaring loudly, "If I don't get my way with the administration, then I'm going to move." Or, failing to get the pay raise he thinks he deserves, he will tell an administrator, "I have to have more money or else I'll leave." The raw reality of the situation soon sobers this type up, else he joins the ranks of the unemployed.

And I have noticed over the years that the professor presenting an either-or ultimatum to the administration had better be prepared to back up his words by taking the "or." I had a friend who tried it once several years ago when the market was still loose; he told the president that, by heaven, he was going to be allowed to start a regional history center at that institution or else he would leave (and he was a fellow of some stature within the field because he had won the Pulitzer Prize). The president stood up, shook his hand, and told him that it had been nice having him on the campus for several years. He even wished my friend good luck at his future institution.

HIRING PROFESSORS

Recently I was in Boston as a consultant to one of the "think tanks," working on a project related to my field. At that august institution I met several doctoral candidates from Harvard and fell to discussing the job market with them. "How many were placed this year?" I asked.

Faces fell into a pattern of deep gloom. "So far about 12 percent in the History Department," I was told. One of them told me that many graduate students in that area were stretching out their work an extra two or three years in the hope that the market would improve (that is, slowing down to do a year's work in two years or a year and a half's work in three years). Of course, they asked how our history graduates did at my institution.

I was able to tell them truthfully, "We placed 100 percent of our doctoral students." All of them did get jobs, although some were in historical administration (historical society work); but the majority did get teaching positions in colleges. And that was not in junior colleges. All went to work at four-year institutions.

I have never seen such looks of incredulity as were on the faces of the Harvard graduate students there in Boston. I could see fleeting looks of disbelief, but when I named the schools that had hired our graduates the disbelief changed to something else, a combination of hatred and of wondering. I am certain that the question in all their minds was one they could not ask without openly admitting the snobbery that all of them feel: How could a Midwestern university, one granting the doctorate in history for only four or five years, place 100 percent and Harvard do so poorly? Or, to put it another way, who in his right mind would hire a professor from a Midwestern cow college when he could get a Harvard man for the same price?

I could have explained to these poor souls the answers, but those would not have comforted New England Brahmans. During the boom times of the late 1950s and most of the 1960s the only Ivy League Ph.D.'s to move out in the hinterlands and take employment were the third-rate types. The good ones—if there are such graduates of these schools, which I often doubt—stayed in the region at the local institutions of higher learning; the poor ones moved west and south because they could not obtain employment at home and because a doctorate from an Ivy League institution did have some prestige. Small institutions in the South, the Midwest, the Southwest, and the Pacific Coast region did mistakenly hire these people in the vain hope that having professors from Ivy League schools would bring luster to them. Moreover, in much of the region west of the Mississippi River, there is a feeling, a hangover from pioneer days, that everything good comes from the East. Those pioneers bought all their manufactured goods from that region until they became convinced that anything from back East was good and everything local was bad. Those days have been gone for many years now, especially in the case of people.

For three hundred years now the best and brightest, the most ambitious people in the East have pulled up stakes and moved west. That has left only the dull, unimaginative, and unambitious in the region to perpetuate the race; little wonder today that most people in that region are so unappealing. I do recognize that there still are a few bright, imaginative, ambitious ones born in that region, but very few; three centuries of selective downbreeding have done their work too well.

Today those Ivy League types who do come out to Iowa or Texas or Wyoming, the ones who cannot find employment at home, look down their noses at the local yokels. "What clods these Okies are," they said in the 1960s when they were hired there—and lived out of their suitcases and waited for Harvard to call them back. They never tried to become part of the local community or to understand the worth of the local citizens; instead they took local money without giving anything in return and then left a Midwestern or Southern university, even one with a graduate program, to go back to Long Island Community College or some such. Instead of being grateful for employment while out in the hinterlands and trying to do a good job, too many of them have acted smugly superior. I even have known some of them who, while in this region, have refused to give a grade higher than a B or a C, saying in effect that no one from south of the Charles River or west of the Hudson could meet the high standards of the Ivy League.

When I was in graduate school we had one of those types, a Princeton man. He was one of the first hippies, strutting around campus in a pair of cut-off trousers and what looked like homemade shoes, along with a shirt of doubtful ancestry. He taught the history of science while gestating a book some fifteen years in the borning. However, when ten students did sign up for his history of science class, he would award about one B, two or three would get a C, four or five a D, and the rest F. The result was that some five years had to pass before all the upper division and graduate students forgot about his grading scale, and then the class would get another ten sheep. In between he taught nothing but the American history survey course.

Of course there are some of these Harvard and Princeton and Yale types who never get invited back to Brooklyn Night

Community College. Students on almost any campus can point out one of the species. They are bitter, depressed, cynical—and students stay away from them in droves. Therefore they end up teaching nothing but the required freshman classes, which the students have no choice but to take if they wish to graduate. And there the Ivy Leaguer does the maximum damage. He turns off the very students that he should be turning on.

Because of these practices, so widespread in the past, employers in the rest of the country shy away from these intellectual snobs. This just when the job market has dried up to the point that the Ivy Leaguers suddenly have discovered that they need these openings. Now, as a department head, I get bundles of applications from Eastern schools; each year they, along with Big Ten and Pacific Coast schools, send out notices of the qualifications of all their graduates and imply that if we have openings we should look through, take our pick, and hire the man. But we no longer want or need them, and thus their unemployment rate is high. We send them a form letter which in effect says, "Don't call us. We'll call you." Really, this kind of reminds me of a girl who has had a certain boy courting her for years and she kept putting him off; then, when she suddenly finds she wants him, it is to find out that he has married someone else. The marriage now is one between Midwestern schools and Midwestern graduate schools; the boy next door is more appealing than the lad from the Ivy Leagues. (I might add here, as an aside, one other thought about the Ivy League schools. There they have what might be called intellectual carpetbaggers: professors of, let us say, Western American history who have never been west of the Hudson except to deliver a paper to some benighted group of yokels out in the hinterlands; but they sit in this name school or that one and write so learnedly about the region—which they know very little about. Carpetbaggers of a new stripe!)

Another rule of thumb I have discovered here in the interior of the country is never to hire someone whose home and training have been near an ocean. Characters raised near the sea have a lemming-like obsession with salt water, perhaps something primordial, that demands that they go down to the ocean at every opportunity. If you hire one of these types at an institution some distance from their salty home and are hoping for permanency, you will be disappointed. Before you know it, he will find some way to get employed nearer the sea. The rule of thumb seems to be, if you want permanency hire someone from a region similar to your own.

Finally—and this is strictly a personal bias—I prefer to hire Southerners. As a professor once explained to me, people from the South have suffered more than Northerners and thus have greater humanity; for this reason they make better teachers. Moreover, their brand of ignorance is of a higher grade, higher quality ignorance than can be found among Northerners. When you go to hire a professor, the question is not whether he will be ignorant but rather what is the caliber of his ignorance—and Southerners have the best kind.

The best rule of thumb is never to hire a professor, but if you must do so then hire a Southerner who lives as far from the sea as possible.

MAIL-ORDER DIPLOMAS

In the spring of 1973, after the appearance of the first Professor X book, I was in New York City to do some television talk shows to promote the work. On one of these, the producer brought in from a local institution of good repute a professor of philosophy who was supposed to demolish me. And that fellow was perfectly cast for the role, for he showed up in rumpled suit, hair askew, and curved-stem pipe furiously billowing smoke. He pointed out that I was wrong about professors; that most of them were hard-working and underpaid for doing an excellent job, that to become a professor took the equivalent of seven years of study, and that professors should not be attacked but revered.

When finally I was able to get a word in sideways, I asked

him why, if professing was such a demanding job, that the Great Imposter was able to walk in off the street without any training whatsoever and get a position as a professor of philosophy. To my surprise the audience there broke into applause (I subsequently learned that the extent of the hostility of the public to professors was such that I was playing to a sympathetic audience).

And it is true that this fellow, the Great Imposter, was able to pass himself off, among other things, as a doctor, a prison warden, a monk, and a professor of philosophy. I believe there even was a movie based on the man's life with no less than Tony Curtis playing the lead. When he secured that academic position in a philosophy department, I don't know how he managed to send in his credentials (here I inject a note that when a would-be professor applies for an academic position, he has to send in copies of his transcripts to show at what institutions he studied, the grades he received, and the degrees he was awarded). Perhaps this Great Imposter made up his own transcripts, or perhaps he somehow managed to avoid sending any in. At any rate, academicians were duly horrified that he was able to pass himself off so easily.

Actually this antic does not surprise me. I firmly believe that I could take in off the street almost anyone of average or slightly above-average intelligence no matter how little college education he has had, and in three or four months I could pass him off as a professor at almost any institution in the land. By having him observe in the classroom a few times, showing him how so many professors crib lectures, and drilling him a little on the catchwords now current, I believe he would do all right.

Nor would I have to forge a fake transcript for him, for there are mailorder institutions of higher learning where for a few hundred dollars he could get a degree or even three of them. These exist in several states, but particularly in the South; I guess the confidence men who run these frauds prefer the sunshine while conducting their business. These exist under several names—Upstairs University, Second Floor College, or some such; in fact, many of the names are very high sounding: The Great All-American University, etc.

Advertisements for these institutions appear in newspapers, the classified section of some magazines, even occasionally in academic journals: "Enrollments now being taken for advanced degrees. Earn your Ph.D in three months." You answer one of these and they send you an application immediately. For a fee ranging from $250 to $2,500, you are allowed to earn your doctorate of philosophy degree by filling in the application blank; this automatically enrolls you in a complete course of study, gets your grades assigned, and brings you through the mail a diploma suitable for framing.

A few of the really high class mail-order institutions make you wait three months, and then you have to fly down to the home university (staying in their facilities for a week) to pass a comprehensive examination. If you fail, you pay a few hundred dollars more for "remedial tutoring," and then you pass. Now what could be simpler than that? Why bother to study seven years at some regular institution, an experience that will cost you thousands and thousands of dollars, when you can go to one of these and be an instant Ph.D?

These institutions apparently do enough business to make the things profitable, for the ads continue to run where they will be seen. There always are a few egotists around who want to frame a diploma awarding them a Ph.D.—and who are willing to pay for the privilege. I recall a few years ago one such institution was shut down by the authorities in Texas, a move that brought wide publicity—and which caused three or four county school superintendents in a neighboring state to resign in a hurry when it became known that their only schooling was from that tainted institution.

On this question of fraudulent degrees, there is another side to the business: the awarding of "honorary" degrees by regularly accredited institutions of higher learning. This practice originated to give public recognition to those rare individuals who made outstanding contributions to human knowledge. Someone who wrote great books might be awarded a Doctorate of Letters or a Doctorate of Literature; a politician that the institution wanted to indicate was a statesman was given a Doctorate of Law degree; and the preacher who was to be made a theologian was given a Doctorate of Divinity.

The theory behind such degrees was laudable, for society should have some way of honoring its great men. However, human nature being what it is, the privilege was abused in short order. To be elected governor was to be certain of getting an honorary degree or two from institutions of higher learning that aspired to a bigger budget, while the fellow who could lay a larger sum on some institution certainly qualified to become a doctorate of something or other. So most states passed laws forbidding the state colleges and universities from passing out honorary degrees. Now these institutions have to give out "Distinguished Service Awards" and, if the donor or politician being courted happens to be a graduate of that institution, he is awarded a "Distinguished Alumnus" certificate.

I really don't have too much of a fuss to make about these new designations, for anyone who gives a sizeable sum to higher education should be recognized in some substantive way. But these awards and certificates should be given after the fact and not before as a way of courting a gift.

If the various state institutions no longer can give honorary doctorates, however, the many private colleges and universities are not so restricted—and the sale of honorary degrees is about all that is keeping some of these schools solvent. The going price these days, I understand, is about $100,000 for an honorary degree from the better schools still engaged in this practice.

Finally, I come to the small church colleges that are just barely holding students and faculty together. There at every commencement the college awards five or six Doctor of Divinity degrees to preachers in the vicinity. These are ministers whose churches make a steady donation to keep the institution going. A president of one of these schools, an honest fellow, told me that without these donations he would have had to close his institution. And, he said, he always made sure that he required a preacher aspiring to an honorary doctor's degree to have his church make at least a $5,000 donation for at least five years before giving the degree, for he had noted that the minute most preachers got an honorary doctorate they stopped the annual contribution. "They no longer want anything to do with us, no connection," this president told me, "for they are embarrassed at how they obtained the degree."

I might add that these preachers are not too embarrassed by the process to ignore their new stature. Whenever one of them gets such a degree, he immediately instructs his staff and his faithful congregation to address him as "Doctor." And he changes his title on the bulletin board outside the church and on the printed literature of the church from "Reverend" to "Doctor." I know one who immediately had new business cards printed for himself with his new title on them. Ah, vanity, vanity. If you think this is an exaggeration, the next time you are introduced to a preacher carrying the title of Doctor, ask him what kind of doctorate it is; the odds are he will say a Doctorate of Divinity. And on the bulletin board outside, it will say Reverend so-and-so, D.D. (D.D. is the abbreviation for Doctorate of Divinity).

There are occasions, however, when the practice of honorary doctorates do come in handy for institutions of higher learning. Years ago I was teaching at a major university in that region of the country whose president had only one academic degree, a bachelor of shop education; he held his position by virtue of his rank of major general in the state national guard and the fact that this school was heavily military in emphasis. Nearby was a name university run by a protestant sect; its president likewise had no doctorate of any type, but held his position by virtue of his orthodox beliefs (and possibly some shrewd politicking). The absence of a doctorate for these presidents was an embarrassment to both institutions, so they arranged a swap; each would deliver the commencement address at the other's school and be awarded an honorary doctorate of letters. Our own leader, the major general, went up to the other school and lectured the troops without benefit of a written speech. I mercifully refrain from describing more about that day. But he returned to our hallowed halls of ivy crowned with his doctorate, and thereafter we could address him with the comfortable title of Doctor.

So there it is. If you aspire to a doctor's degree but do not wish to give up seven years of your life to earn it, you have two choices. Either make some great discovery, write some great book, perform some great deed, and you will pick up an honorary doctorate; or make enough money to lay about $100,000 on the college that still sells these degrees—you will have no real problem finding one—and it will put a cap and gown on you. In fact, if you shop around a little, I suspect you will find an institution that even will frame your diploma for you, thus saving you that expense.

AFFIRMATIVE ACTION

There now stalks the land of higher education an ogre called Affirmative Action, a creation of bureaucrats in Washington who have determined to remake the country in the social image they desire. These bureaucrats are third-echelon types entrenched in the Civil Service and have the equivalent of tenure; no president can really dictate to these people, for they cannot be fired, and they have decided they know what is best for universities and colleges.

What is best apparently is the same quota system applied to the Democratic Party in the election of 1972 when half the delegates had to be female, a certain percentage black, another set percentage young, etc. Translated into higher educational terms, Affirmative Action as decreed by these wise men of Washington means that if 12 percent of all Ph.D.s in the discipline of chemistry are female, then all departments of chemistry in the United States must have 12 percent females on their staff; and if 5 percent of all Ph.D.s in chemistry are black, then every department of chemistry in the United

States must have 5 percent blacks on its staff. The same with Indians and Orientals and Mexican-Americans. There is no taking into account the personality factor—that a Chicano who applies for a job at your institution might not fit in or that his personality may be such that you don't want him. You must hire this percentage.

In recent months the number of Affirmative Action forms that have crossed my desk is astonishing. I have spent the equivalent of seven or eight full working days filling out these things—which make about as much sense as you would expect a government form to make. For example, one of these wanted to know the exact qualifications for every rank in my department, from graduate assistant to part-time instructor to full professor, even for department head. Then on each of these gems I had to show where I recruited these people. Mind you, some of my faculty came here almost before I was born, but nevertheless I had to say why a black or a female was not hired for that position. Moreover, I had to state how many minority people and females were available at that time for those positions. And I had to give the source of my information. I could not say, "not available" or "I don't know"; I had to give some exact source.

Somehow I struggled through the thing, only to receive within a week another form requiring me to state how many openings I would have in the next five years in each of the categories of employment in my department. Inasmuch as no crystal ball came with the job, how the hell do I know? But I put down something. Then, below that, was a pledge form (shades of my church and its annual pledge card); I had to indicate how many minority and female professors I pledged to hire within the next five years. These all were compiled by the dean's office, and an announcement came in due time that the college of arts and sciences had pledged to hire x number of blacks, x number of Chicanos, x number of orientals, and x number of females in the next five years. Of course, we will be lucky to have that many openings in the next five years, but I suspect that the goal will be met if possible—else we

33

will have several more visits by the Affirmative Action people on our campus, something not exactly relished by anyone in his right mind.

It no longer is acceptable to these bureaucrats to advertise that you have an opening, that you went through the applicants, and that you picked the most qualified man, the one who seemed most likely to do the job you want. No, you now must be able to demonstrate "Affirmative Action." This means that you must advertise the job—and keep copies of the ads—in places likely to be seen by minorities and females. You must ask on every application what race and sex the job seeker is. You must make notes of all telephone conversations relating to the position: whom you called or who called you, what was the nature of the conversation, and did you state clearly that you are actively seeking minority and female applicants for the position? And every letter you write about the position must state that your university is an "equal opportunity employer."

Moreover, when at last you do recommend to your administration that a certain person be hired to fill the position, you must fill out an "Affirmative Action" report. How many blacks applied for this position? How many Indians? How many orientals? How many females? How many Mexican-Americans? I must list my first, second, and third choices for the position, and I must affirm that I took positive action to secure a minority or female person for the position.

Of course, the result of all this coercion—and that is the only word for it—is that most of us take the easy way out and hire a minority person or female no matter whether that person really fits what we need. And this at a time when the job market is extremely tough. In my own field of history, for example, the American Historical Association reported that for the year 1973 only some 54 percent of those who graduated with Ph.D. in history were employed in the profession. In this time of few jobs, the only ones getting employed are the females and minority types.

Now I am a firm believer in equality—of opportunity. I

hold as a strong tenet of faith that the best person ought to be hired to fill any position that is open, and that no one should be discriminated against because of sex or race. But the raw truth now is that every white, male student (I did not add Anglo-Saxon and Protestant to this list because even being Jewish no longer is good enough to get a job or to be cheated out of it) in graduate school ought to be told by his adviser to take a course in taxi driving or manual labor. The few jobs that are available are closed to him because of his sex and race.

With bureaucrats like that running around, it is no wonder that the hard hats of America are conservative. This is about the only job a white male can get in this country any more, Ph.D. or no Ph.D. The hard hats are bitter—and with good reason.

When these liberal bureaucrats are told that they are now practicing reverse discrimination on the basis of sex and race, they say it is necessary to balance past wrongs. Well, down in the part of the country where I grew up, the preachers always said, "Two wrongs don't make a right." I don't see how we reverse the past trend of racism and sexism by practicing a new brand.

There are other contradictions built into the present situation. In this era when we *have* to hire minorities and females, when we *have* to promote them first and give them outsize pay raises, else be convicted or racism and sexism, we are violating the academic freedom of white male professors and aspiring professors. And the civil libertarians and members of the American Association of University Professors who claim to have been fighting so long for academic freedom stand for the new order—which violates the academic freedom they claim to want: the forced hiring and promotion of any one group on the basis of sex and race violates academic freedom. But this type goes on blithely, proclaiming that he stands for academic freedom *and* the new order of hiring and promotion and pay raises.

Another concomitant of Affirmative Action is that it has

stripped most small black colleges and universities of their best and brightest faculty. The competition is on among all schools everywhere because of these new federal guidelines and programs to hire blacks. There are very few qualified blacks in the country (and I will not argue the point that in the past they were not encouraged to go on). Thus white colleges and universities shamelessly raid the black schools of their best faculty members—when these are the very people who should be teaching at these institutions.

And because blacks as well as other minorities—the qualified ones—are in such strong demand, they can get higher starting salaries than equally qualified whites, which is another kind of discrimination. Well, if I were black, I would no doubt think all of this a good thing and make the most of it. In fact, that is what I tell my black graduate students. Get the Ph.D. and make the most of the present situation! Work hard, learn to be the best in the business, and take the present opportunities. But I wish these federal bureaucrats would tell me what to say to my white male graduate students!

Moreover, I resent that I am automatically considered guilty of racism, bigotry, and male chauvinism when I hire someone not black and/or female. In the present situation if I do not hire a minority person or female, I am considered guilty until I prove myself innocent, which is not the way I understand the law. And even if I do prove that I did not practice racism and sexism, the image still lingers. The only way to avoid ending up in court, it seems, is to hire the minority or female applicant even if he/she is underqualified (and the way hair is these days, it sometimes is difficult to tell the difference; moreover, if you smell some of these people, you don't even care to know the difference).

Ah, well, in this brave new world in which we live, I suppose everyone should have an equal opportunity to teach in a college in order not to work for a living. What really worries me is that once these bureaucrats finish with us, they will start in an other occupations. I was lamenting the new regulations to a college traveler for one of the book publishers the other day, and he laughed hard at my predicament. Just for fun I asked him, "What are the minimum qualifications for your job?"

He stopped chuckling and said, "About all that is necessary is that you be breathing."

"And how many of your sales staff are female?" I wanted to know.

"We have two women."

"How many salesmen are traveling for your house?" I wanted to know.

"Twenty-four," he replied.

"Any blacks?"

"No."

"Well," I said, "when the Affirmative Action people finish with us, they will be down to see your sales manager to find out why twelve of your people are not women; after all, women do constitute half the population. And there should be at least three or four blacks, because they constitute about 14 percent of the population. That's to say nothing about Mexican-Americans, Indians, and orientals. Oh, you can bet that the Affirmative Action people will be around to see you."

The salesman left, not finding much humor in my predicament.

LANDING EMPLOYMENT

How well I remember my first interview for a job as a professor. It was at a small, fundamentalist, denominational college, and the dean looked like God's agent here on earth. I sat there uncomfortably listening for what seemed like hours, but which really was about 30 minutes, as he told me about the joys of working at that institution. I finally concluded that they did not pay much money, but that they did guarantee high marks with the Man upstairs and that after forty years there I would certainly get into heaven.

Finally I pulled out a cigarette and looked about for an ash-tray. Seeing this the dean told me, "We don't smoke on our campus." Then, almost visibly wincing, he added, "Well, we did liberalize this year. You can now go into the men's room and sit in one of the cubicles and smoke."

Today I would urge one of my graduate students to take that position, although I ran from it, because a job—any job—is almost impossible to get. In fact, even getting an interview for a job takes more hard work than it once took to get employed at Harvard.

Today the doctoral candidate about to graduate tries to snare employment through several means. He can go to the many conventions within his own discipline at the state, regional, and national level and try to find a department head looking for a faculty member. So many aspiring instructors take this route, however, that I have heard conventions referred to as "the slave market." Many of these conventions maintain what laughingly is called a "Placement Service," but which nowadays is a listing of those looking for work; few use the service to list openings for fear of being mobbed. I heard recently of a national meeting within my own area of history where there were more than 1,700 signed up seeking employment and only four positions listed. Moreover, I had a department head tell me he never again would list an opening there because he had just spent three days sitting in his hotel room interviewing a new candidate every twenty minutes—and never did get around to interviewing everyone who wanted to talk with him.

Another way the finishing graduate student hears of prospective jobs is through the bulletins issued by the national association in his discipline. The American Historical Association, for example, issues a bulletin periodically in which it lists what jobs are available for historians. Because so few jobs are available to the many aspirants, however, all an advertisement does is confuse the institution seeking to hire someone; it takes weeks to look in the most cursory way through all the mail that comes in.

And the young person looking for a job may hear of some opening through friends, if he has any, or from former graduates of the institution where he is studying. In fact, some universities instruct all their graduates, as they are leaving, to write back the minute they hear of an opening somewhere; and if a job should open within their own department at whatever institution they are at, they are to fight to get that place to hire yet another of the old alma mater's graduates. The University of Wisconsin's graduates have been notorious for this practice, which in academe is known openly as the "Big Red Machine." That is why you rarely find Wisconsin grads singly; they ususally are found in nests.

Finally—and I probably should have listed this first—the young man about to cross the commencement stage to receive his doctorate should hear about prospective jobs from his major adviser. Such men are supposed to be mature scholars of such reputation that they can place their graduate students; thus he is supposed to have friends about the country who will tell him about openings, he tells his students, and they apply. However, few of these advisers realize that the job situation has changed drastically, and thus they sit there waiting for the telephone to ring—while their graduate students drive taxis and wait.

As the number of unemployed Ph.Ds grows each year, however, the departments training them are gradually realizing that times have changed, and now we have that wonder of wonders at many doctoral-granting institutions, the Placement Committee. These usually know as much collectively as the members know individually, which is to say nothing. About all they have come up with is the mimeographed list of the department's students who wish a job; this they send out to every institution in the country. Hardly a day goes by but what I receive at least one of these; in fact, so many of the things come in that I never read them anymore. But there is one of these things I believe I will cherish forever; recently I received one from a prestigious Eastern university entitled *The Seed Catalog*. I suppose the implication was that if you would hire one of their young sprouts, he would grow into a mighty oak or some such.

Now, for the mature scholar who tires of his present institution—or, more often, decides he really is too good for the place—the problem of moving is somewhat different. He also hears of what he believes to be a better job, one more worthy of himself then his present position, at conventions or from friends. And, strangely, there are more openings now at the top than at the bottom. Full professors reach the retirement age chronologically (some of them hit the retirement age physically several years before) and have to quit; the institution at which they are working often wishes to hire someone at the full professor level, someone who can direct graduate students, and thus it seeks some mature scholar.

Sometimes such an institution will decide on the man it wants, someone with sufficient stature to attract its attention, and it will approach the individual. Usually this is done by indirection. That is, someone from that school does not go to the scholar and say, "Hey, would you like to come work for us?" Rather, the administration at the school will have some third party approach the scholar and ask, "Would you, if offered a professorship at X university at X salary, be interested in moving?" To make a direct offer without this approach is to run the risk of a public turndown if the scholar says no. In other words, a top job at a name university is never offered directly to someone until the administration at that university is certain he is going to accept it; no one wants his school to be embarrassed by someone not wanting to come there.

Of course, there always is the chance that a scholar approached by some third party will indicate a willingness to move only to get a genuine offer. This he then uses to show his dean and get his salary raised at his present school, after which he turns down the new offer—and thus embarrasses those making the offer.

Some scholars specialize in this, especially those with "academic sex appeal." They generate an offer, one in writing, and then, this in hand, they approach their dean and say,

"Look, that university wants me and is willing to pay me $2,000 (or whatever sum) more than I am making here. I really would like to stay here, but their offer is terribly attractive financially." This kind of power play has to be handled delicately if the professor genuinely wants to stay at his present institution; he has to balance his threat to leave with his open desire to stay, else he may get a handshake and a wave good-bye—and then he has to move.

Or, even worse to someone really doing this only to get a pay raise, he may be told by his dean, "We want you to stay, but we can't raise your salary at this time." This is bad, for if the professor doesn't leave, his administrators know that they have him where they want him and they will give him only token raises thereafter. The good professor must never get into a position where his administration knows it has him "bought and paid for."

What I am saying here is that negotiating for a top-name scholar has to be handled very carefully, else the administration will end up with egg on its face. You have to negotiate carefully and be very certain of your man, else you suffer public embarrassment. The whole thing reminds me of the talk of "face" among the Chinese; both professors and administrators do not want to lose face.

Once the mature or the beginning scholar makes contact with someone with a job to offer, the next step is sending in his credentials, his *vita,* and his letters of recommendation. By credentials I mean transcripts from all the colleges he attended, while the *vita* is a listing of biographical information about himself; and people do lie on these things—or at least make them sound very positive. He does not put down that he is living with his third wife; he merely says "married." He does not say that he was dishonorably discharged from the army; he merely lists "military service, 1968-1970." And he lists all the publications he can here; I have seen these things showing, under publications, such things as "Curriculum Guide" for a course the man teaches, and the publisher is the departmental mimeograph machine.

Then come the letters of recommendation. These are not sent by the candidate himself; rather he lists three or four people to whom the prospective employer might write. Only a fool would list people to be contacted other than his trusted friends; we all expect our friends to lie for us, knowing all too often that our enemies will tell the truth. The fellow looking for his first academic position lists the man who was his major adviser in graduate school, for this man is obligated to help him find a job (in short, he is supposed to put his student in the most favorable possible light—if not lie outright); and he lists a couple of other professors under whom he studied. Inasmuch as these letters all will be from people trying to get the young man employed, the prospective employer should look for very glowing letters. You know the kind I mean: "Mr. Jones, while he studied under me was hard working, cheerful, cooperative, positive, loved students, researched well, and writes like Hemingway." One "however" on these letters and the candidate is dead.

But the prospective employer really has to read the letters about mature scholars even more closely. One who says, "We heartily recommend Mr. Jones," can also be saying, "We hope you take him." Or the one that says, "Professor Jones is a man of genuine ability who, with proper direction, can be a valuable asset," really is saying he is a troublemaker the previous institution could not control. Too glowing a letter about some fellow from his previous employers makes you wonder if they are trying to unload someone on you, while a really bad letter of recommendation can be written about a professor the institution wants to keep without raising his salary.

It is because letters of recommendation and *vita* sheets give only a murky image of the prospective employee that most institutions now insist on bringing these candidates in for a personal interview. The candidate is asked to meet with the department, with the dean, even in some cases with the students. There are many techniques to the interview, but the candidate most has to watch for the kind where his host gives the appearance of being his best friend, the one fighting for him to get the job, and invites confidences: "Tell me, old buddy, what do you really think about all this?" He draws you out until you say something damaging and then uses this against you.

My advice for those going on an academic interview is to take a few pages out of a salesman's manual and tell the prospective employer what he wants to hear. "Boy, this is a great region of the country. I'd really love to work at so fine an institution." The way the job market is these days, any candidate for a position can say truthfully that he would love to work at "so fine an institution," because any place that will hire him has to be great. When the employer asks what courses he can teach, he should reply, 'Why, I'd be happy to teach whatever you feel I am qualified to teach." In short, he should be the most agreeable fellow on earth, and he should hold up a mirror that allows the employer to see exactly what he wants to see.

Employers, meanwhile, have to try to crack the mirror in order to see what the fellow behind it really is like. Once the man gets a contract and knows he is employed, what will he be like? Will he continue to be as pleasant after the contract as he is during the interview?

Employers at universities and colleges know they have to take such a long, hard look nowadays because once they hire a man it is virtually impossible to get rid of him. Firing a professor these days has become next to impossible.

ROLE PLAYING

"Well, this old boy would never look you in the eye. He sorta squinted and turned his head sideways and looked off, just glancin' at you ever' now and then." A friend of mine was describing a professor he knew at another college. "This feller wore nothin' but suits all day," he continued, "but you catch him of an evenin' and he was dressed in regular clothes. Had on his boots and an old blue work shirt and would be out ridin' his horse. Seems he was born on a ranch and loved to ride. But, boy, you catch him around the campus and he was dressed just like some New Yorker."

What my friend was describing is a common phenomenon around college campuses. Professors, especially new ones, try to play the role of university teachers. Psychologists often have commented about role playing and how each of us has to do it. By this they mean we fall into certain patterns of conduct in everyday life, assuming and discarding roles almost like hats; to our children we play the role of parent, to our spouses we play yet another, with our friends yet another, etc. And as we assume these roles, we do so on the basis of what society expects of us, not on our disposition alone. Of course, each of us brings to these roles our own personality and habits, so there are variations; yet there are many similarities.

The trouble with young, newly hired professors is that there is no good, solid role for their chosen line of work. All of them have heard and most have come to believe that professing is one of the last bastions of individualism, so they feel uncomfortable when they try to become Mr. College Instructor. The way most of them get around that dilemma is to assume the posture, coloration, dress, and attitudes of the men under whom they studied in graduate school. They dress like them, talk like them, act like them, even grade like them.

But this action, entirely understandable and totally human, often gets them in trouble. You see, they study at some big university where the role of professor is entirely different from what is at the small school where most young men first get employed. The newly hired assistant professor arrives at the junior college, private four-year institution, or state college devoted to training teachers, and finds that his big-university image isolates him from his students, causes the old hands to distrust him as a snob, or else leads everyone to believe he is trying to leave as fast as possible. And that is what most of the young ones do—try to leave as fast as possible, because they feel cheated. To themselves they say, "I am acting like a professor is supposed to act, yet no one appreciates me." Ergo, this place must be bad. So he searches for another position. If he doesn't find it, then he stays—to become surly, defensive, critical of his students, contemptuous of his colleagues, full of hatred for the administration, and full of disdain for the region. Little does he realize that when all this happens, he at last has assumed the role played by too many professors.

I have watched graduate students over the years, budding professors, groping to find a handle to the role of college instructor. Some of them, as I stated above, ape their advisers— and this does get them through. The adviser feels complimented to see himself in his students; it reinforces his own belief in his superiority, feeds his ego, and strengthens his prejudices. I have often wondered if graduate students and their advisers tend to be similar because likes attract or because the student assumes the same role as his adviser. I notice that professors who are S.O.B.s have S.O.B.s for graduate students, and good-old-boy profs have good-old-boy graduate students, and working members of the graduate faculty have workers studying under them. I guess this is the old chicken-and-egg argument and can never be resolved fully.

Yet this similarity between graduate student and adviser can have tragic consequences. I know one man, a full professor now, who when a graduate student began playing the role of professor to the hilt. He always dressed in a coat and tie, albeit somewhat tweedy, even a little seedy; he puffed judiciously on his pipe before answering anything; when asked any question, he answered that he would have to make a study of all the evidence before rendering a verdict; and when he did speak, it was in heavy, measured tones that implied he was merely a loudspeaker for words from heavy. This behavior got him through graduate school easily. The same behavior eventually brought him to a mid-sized university with a graduate program.

However, this individual today is a frustrated person, for this behavior has not brought him the fame and renown he seeks. He still talks as if a mouthpiece for God, he dresses like a professor should dress, he sits in his office with his door closed, always working furiously on some big project that never results in publication; he brings reams of "research" to answer the most trivial question. But he has not published. He has not learned that students have changed in the last decade and a half, that they will not tolerate the make-work assignments which their fathers and mothers performed without murmur.

Today this man sits with diminishing enrollments, no great fame among his colleagues—and wonders what happened. What went wrong? Even some of the professors who trained him wonder the same thing. I ran into one at a convention, and we fell to discussing the man. "We can't figure it out," said the professor who had been a member of the fellow's doctoral committee. "We expected more from him than from almost anyone else we've trained. But he hasn't done anything." (I report this conversation correctly despite what you may think; professors *do* in casual conversations speak in contractions.)

The tragedy of this man's career is that he assumed a role that got him through graduate school, got him employed, and even got him promoted. However, he failed to discern that somewhere along the way he had to quit playing a role and go to work. Or that it was fine to play a role, but that changing times force a change in roles. Most professors do get by without working, but they do change roles. I watch this breed with fascination. They are the ones capable of bandying about all the latest catch-phrases of educational jargon; they keep up with the latest fashions and fads among intellectuals; they pander to students sufficiently to keep their enrollments up. But they never work.

Finally, on this matter of playing the professorial role, I note that the public image of the professor has changed. In the not-so-distant past the professor was regarded as lovable if absent-minded. In fact, it seemed impossible to say the word professor without adding absent-minded—as if all three words constituted only one. One of the men under whom I studied was the epitome of this type. On one occasion he took his car to a football game a hundred miles distant, then caught the train home. Failing to find his auto at home, he reported to the police that it had been stolen. They found it in the parking lot of the stadium a hundred miles away and told him he could retrieve it there. According to the legend, he went down to the train station to go get his car—and bought a round-trip ticket.

I was curious if this story were true and asked him about it. "No," he replied, "that's not true. I only bought a one-way-ticket to go get it."

Yet this old man, for all his faults of absent-mindedness, was a remarkable professor. Another story about him held that one day he arrived in class to begin a lecture only to discover that he could not find his notes. He searched through all his pockets, looked all around the podium, even stirred the mouldy contents of his briefcase. Then to the class he said, "I guess we can't have class today. I can't find my notes." However, as he started toward the door, he looked down to the floor. "Wait," he told the students, "We can have class. Here're my notes." He picked up a three-by-five note card on which he had written two words: Queen Victoria. Picking that up, he proceeded to give a startlingly good fifty-minute lecture about the reign of that British monarch.

I was talking with him about this and he admitted the truth of the legend. "Usually," he said, "I jot my lecture notes just before class. I put them on the first sheet of a typing pad, and at the end of class I tear that sheet out and throw it away. This keeps me young. I don't read the same lectures year after year like some I know." He and I both knew which professors on the staff he was referring to, for the yellow-note syndrome was notorious—people who had not revised or updated lectures in years.

Today, however, the image of the professor no longer is that of the lovable but absent-minded individual. I haven't heard the adjective "lovable" applied to professors in many years. Crazy, yes. Fuzzy-headed liberals, yes. Several other adjectives that are unprintable, yes!

For the young professor worried about his image and the role he should play, my advice is to be himself. "To thine own self be true . . . " is still good advice. The students appreciate honesty and truthfulness and will like you better for it. The problem is that too many young professors do not know—or want to forget—who they are. The problems of the young college instructor are those of our nation as a whole: affluence, sloth, shame at our humble origins. Sadly, too much of what I write is not aimed solely at professorial nature, but rather at human nature. Nothing is wrong with the country that old-fashioned hard work and honesty will not cure.

The trick to graduate school—and even life itself—is, when you are sweating to get through, reflect back what the profs want to see, but in the process never sell out the essential you. Inside, where you live, hang on to your beliefs. Too many people reflect what the professors of life want to see until they forget who they are and where they came from. You always should hang on to this, for it is the very thing which makes you yourself.

FIRING PROFESSORS

In higher education today we have artists who cannot draw, musicians who cannot compose, English teachers who cannot write, psychologists who are sick in the head, economists who do not understand the capitalist system, and historians with no feeling for the past—to say nothing of political scientists who want to overthrow the American system of government, humanities professors whose only qualification is to have failed in the ministry, and educationists who do not know how to teach.

At the same time we are faced with student enrollments which, if they are not declining, have at least leveled off. Nor, looking at the birth rate and high-school enrollments, are we likely to have another large influx of students in the immediate future. As a result we have a surplus of professors—and that is not counting the new ones coming out of graduate school who cannot find jobs. Therefore many schools are faced with the hard prospect of cutting some people from their staff.

This raises the question: how do you get rid of faculty members?

The answer is not easy because of that wondrous thing known as tenure. A faculty member acquires tenure—for want of a better explanation—by breathing a required number of years at some institution. This varies from state to state, but a good average would be about six years for an assistant professor, four for an associate professor, and one for a full professor. Once the faculty member gains tenure he cannot be fired except for cause, something generally interpreted to mean "moral turpitude" (fooling with the coeds).

Until three or four years ago, college and university administrators pointed with pride to the percentage of their faculty that was tenured. Having a faculty that stayed with you year after year was regarded as a positive thing for a school, for a stable faculty indicated an institution where everyone was happy. In fact, administrators bragged about the number of professors who stayed year after year, and one of the first questions they asked about some potential employee was, "Will he stay with us?"

Now, in the changing job market, however, administrators have grown leery of too high a percentage of tenured faculty members and are even searching for some way to set limits on the percentage that can be tenured. Some say that no more than 50 percent of the teachers should be granted tenure, while others believe 60 or even 70 percent is the correct figure. Once this limit, whatever it may be, is reached, no additional faculty members will be granted tenure. Administrators defend this new attitude by saying a certain amount of faculty turnover is necessary in order to get an infusion of new blood and new ideas.

This concept does not strike me right, although I do admit that some faculty members work awfully hard until they get tenure and then they quit (working, not the job). As long as some of them do not have tenure, you will have some who are working. The real problem at schools is not keeping a set per-

49

centage from getting tenure, but rather getting the ones with tenure to work. Perhaps what is needed is tenure for a specified length of time, then reevaluation with the right to another period of tenure. The only other people in America I can think of who have a hold on their jobs equal to what the professors have are the civil service employees of the federal government—and I don't think I need to go into the evils that tenure has produced in both cases.

Rather, the problem now is that some schools have had shrinking enrollments to the point that they have had to cut faculty, including some of the tenured. Recently I saw a story in one of the weekly newspapers devoted to higher education about some state systems (in Illinois and Wisconsin, for example) that had to drop some tenured faculty members. Such news blows through the college teaching ranks like a cold, wintery blast, causing fear to clutch at many incompetent hearts.

Even that militant group known as the American Association of University Professors (abbreviated hereafter as the AAUP), which in the past has set its guidelines for the granting of tenure, has a provision for cutting out jobs no longer needed. According to the AAUP, even a tenured faculty member can be fired if the position he holds is abolished for two years. However, this provision no longer is in favor because the market is not expanding the way it once was, and anyone let go cannot easily find a new job. Therefore tenured faculty members whose jobs have been abolished and who have been let go now are suing more and more colleges. If they win, the implication is obvious: once you hire a professor, you cannot fire him—especially when you note that more and more faculty members are suing when they are denied tenure. If the courts hold that colleges and universities must grant tenure to anyone who is hired and also rule that a tenured faculty member cannot be fired even if his job is abolished, then anyone who hires a prof is stuck with him until he turns sixty-five.

I am not now and never have been a member of the AAUP— nor do I foresee joining that organization. My own feeling always has been that if an institution where I am working does not want me, then I will move. I believe anyone paying a salary to a worker has the right to fire him. Therefore I have always viewed the AAUP as an organization composed of those who, for the most part, fear—and with an intuitive knowledge of their incompetence—for their jobs. They band together for protection, to be joined by idealists and liberals who sympathize with them for misguided reasons.

Because of the way I see this organization, I have been strongly criticized by members of the group—which amounts, on their part, to a denial of my academic freedom. Ah, well, these people have never been famous for their logic.

By way of explanation of my stand, however, let me state that I have been at three schools where a faculty member was terminated for one reason or another, whereupon each filed a protest with the AAUP. In cases such as these the AAUP investigates, takes notes from the accuser and the accused, and then at the next general convention of the organization votes to censure or not to censure the university in question. In all three cases that I witnessed, the AAUP voted to censure the school—when from personal observation I saw that the institution was justified in firing all three of these men. (Censure by the AAUP meant that members of the teaching profession were thereby warned that the institution so labeled was reactionary—or guilty of violating the academic freedom of some faculty member—and that no one should take employment there. Obviously with jobs as scarce as they are at the present, censure by the AAUP has little meaning.)

Never once to my knowledge has an institution been charged with violating someone's academic freedom or due process but that the AAUP has sided with the individual and not with the institution's administration. There may have been instances where this happened, but I have not heard of them. And I would be far more inclined to trust the organization if occasionally it came out in its bulletin and said, "We have investigated the charges against so-and-so university and conclude that the man in question should have been fired." I cannot believe that in every contest between administrator and faculty member that the administrator is guilty and a dirty dog to boot and that the faculty member is innocent and a saint.

An incident which illustrates this point occurred when I was promoting *This Beats Working for a Living*. On one of the television talk shows, the one I mentioned elsewhere in this book about the fellow who charged me with anti-feminine bias, the gentleman questioned me about my attitude toward the AAUP. And he charged me with vilifying the profession needlessly. Finally I asked him, "Have you ever known one—just one—incompetent faculty member anywhere?"

He hemmed and hawed and tried to evade my question, but finally he admitted that he had known a few, a very few, poor professors.

"And did you actively work to get them dismissed from the school at which they were employed? In short, did you try to get them fired or in any way penalized for their incompetence?"

Again, with reluctance, he answered—a weak no. My feelings toward the AAUP would be much higher if I ever saw a case where it tried to get some incompetent out of the profession. Instead, it seems to work with the blind credo that in any given situation the faculty members are right and all administrators (along with all regents and legislators) are wrong. And if you disagree with them, all too many of these types will hound you for your beliefs, even try to shout down your right to free speech—which again is a denial of the academic freedom for which they profess to work. I have found the AAUP excessively concerned with salaries and due process and job tenure, but relatively unconcerned about giving a day's work for a day's pay, or about justice and the rights of employers. In short, I would like to see the organization get less preoccupied with *rights* and far more occupied about *responsibilities*. If that makes me a reactionary, then so be it.

Yet there now are cases where the AAUP actively is seeking to become the bargaining agent for faculty members—in exactly the same way that any union serves as bargaining agent for its members. This is being done under federal labor laws allowing employees at any business to petition and then hold an election to see if some organization is to represent everyone of the employees in bargaining sessions with the management. I hold that such a practice is dangerous to the profession, for if they are going to act like factory workers they may get treated like factory workers; someone from the legislature or the regents may come down to the campus and begin checking on productivity, something most faculty members would not want—and could not stand.

And it seems to me that if some local AAUP chapter wins the right to represent the faculty either by a wide majority or a narrow one, it still thereby would be forcing those who voted against it to have the AAUP represent them. If local chapters of this organization are going to function as labor unions, then they should be as honest as labor unions and drop their academic cant of "academic freedom," admit their true goals, and label the rest of us the "scabs" they believe us to be.

And because of the job shortage, the surplus of professors, and the uncertainty of the future, there now are labor unions forming on certain campuses under a variety of names, most of them rather high-sounding. Hardly an issue of newspapers devoted to higher education crosses my desk but that I see where a vote on unionization and collective bargaining has taken place on some campus or another. This may well be the wave of the future, although I am not certain how well I and those who think like me will fit into this brave, new world.

One acquaintance of mine who became president of a mid-sized Midwestern university, and he was a man of liberal bent, quickly was confronted with a group of professors talking of unionization and collective bargaining. When they came to him about the idea, he told them, "Fine, but remember, the minute we start bargaining, all previous bets are off." Asked to clarify this, he explained that he meant all bargaining started with a clean slate; all previous benefits provided by the university would have to be negotiated, as would retirement salaries, number of hours taught, tenure, etc. (Here allow me to insert that most universities have an attractive fringe-benefit package which includes free medical insurance, free life insurance, a retirement plan, etc.; generally this amounts to at least 15 percent of a faculty member's annual salary, and in some cases as high as 21 percent.)

This particular faculty, faced with renegotiating tenure and work load and fringe benefits, backed hastily away from the notion of unionizing, and since that time have not been back to see the president.

It is my fervent wish that other university presidents and their regents take a similar firm stand. I have no desire to face a choice between leaving the profession and joining a union against my will.

Actually the present situation in which higher education finds itself—too many professors and too few students—would be a good time to upgrade most college faculties. And such might be the case but for the overriding threat of lawsuits. One dean told me, as he rolled his eyes toward heaven, "If I could just abolish tenure for thirty minutes. . . ." But we are living in the age in which it is popular to sue anyone at the drop of a hat, and thus even those institutions where half and more of the faculty has never completed the Ph.D. cannot have them fired, for they were granted tenure in the old days when faculty members were scarce.

The next question that arises, when anyone talks of having to cut some people loose because of declining enrollments, is how to judge faculty performance. In other words, how do you decide which one to fire? One elderly professor told me the question was easily decided. Said he with finality, "Seniority counts!" What he meant was to fire first the man hired last. Naturally such talk of seniority never comes from the Young Turks; rather this is what the Old Guard say. And they do have a point.

Then the Young Turks, many of them not yet having attained tenure and thus still working hard, say, "Productivity is what should count." And they have a legitimate point.

And all, young and old, talk vaguely of merit—only to fall into hopeless argument as to what constitutes merit. Strangely, however, you can walk into almost any department on any campus, and students as well as professors can tell you who is working and who is not (of course, always excluding the man doing the talking from judging himself). And there is surprising unanimity on this point. Good professors stand out, just as do the poor ones. Any competent department head can tell you which of his faculty members is contributing most to the needs of the department, just as he can tell you which of them is hurting the program. Moreover, every good dean knows which of his department heads is doing a good job and which is not. If the dean insisted on good department heads and forced the incompetent ones out, and if the department heads in turn would recommend tenure only for those working hard and likely to continue to do so in the future, all higher education would benefit.

But I have noted that the minute the question of tenure or promotion comes before a group of faculty members—the good, the bad, and the indifferent—they vote for the man with the longest service. Seniority all too often is the criterion for promotion, not merit, work, teaching load, productivity, or contribution. Just having been at an institution and breathing longer than others within the same rank.

What does the future hold? I am not certain, of course, but I do foresee certain trends. I think that in the future tenure will be harder to get. Ten years, not six, will become more common. (I might add that I think promotion also is going to become much harder to get; eight or ten years from assistant to associate professor and from associate to full professor will replace the current four or five years necessary for promotion.) In fact, it would not surprise me to see many institutions going to one-year contracts containing a clause stating there is no guarantee of additional employment. That may become standard for beginning professors; I think it will be done to avoid lawsuits in those cases where a man now is hired for three years and then sues the university because he is not granted tenure.

Another trend I see in the future is an earlier retirement for senior members of the faculty. At most schools the present age for being put out to pasture is sixty-five, although some states allow professors to continue on a year-to-year basis until age seventy. I think that I will be able to retire at age sixty and that this will become fairly common in the future; this will be done to make room for others who want to enjoy the benefits of college professing.

And—hopefully—the profession is going to find some good way of determining merit, else the whole system is going to fall into disrepute and higher education no longer will enjoy the prestige in America that it has in the past. Many institutions in the past equated merit with publications, the "publish or perish" syndrome, but this did not work out too well because, first and foremost, professors are hired to teach. Our salaries come from the state for our classroom performance, not from the products of our pens and typewriters. We must find some effective way of measuring each professor's classroom work and then have the guts to reward the good ones and fire the bad ones.

The great difficulty with this, however, is that once you fire a professor you have to hire another . . . which brings this chapter full circle.

II

The Changing University Scene

LIMITED HORIZONS

Youth is the time to dream great dreams, to think of climbing Kilamanjaro and winning the Indianapolis 500 and playing professional sports. Youth is a time of unlimited horizons, when anything seems possible—and *is* if only one closes his eyes and dreams a bit. (Here I might add that I think a good bit of what is wrong with the country is that children today have too little time to dream. They are over organized. Too many lessons might be classed as the curse of modern childhood. Piano lessons, ballet lessons, horseback riding lessons, cub scouts, brownie scouts—the list is endless. Yet children need time to watch the clouds change shapes and listen to the grass grow and speculate about what it would be like to fly like birds.)

As young people approach college, most of them still dream, but in a more realistic way. Of course, there are still a few who long for the impossible. Society needs a few of these people, for often it is they who accomplish their dreams by climbing a new mountain, establishing some sort of new record. But most of our young settle for more ordinary things. They dream of becoming president of General Motors or International Telephone and Telegraph, or else president of the United States—at least a senator or governor, or perhaps just the best farmer in the county or the richest real estate man in town. For most, it might be said that they have set their goals very high, even excessively high. They dream big dreams, which is good if they set out working hard to achieve these goals. Riches, fame, good fortune—all are expected to be part of the future.

But the young man who aspires to be a college professor has less magnificent dreams. He knows, if he looks at the situation realistically, that the best he can do is to become a full professor and that the top salary is about $25,000. In short, he begins his career with a limited horizon. Lightning is very unlikely to strike and make him a millionaire or a leader of his nation or a captain of industry.

And, just as his economic future is very restricted, so also is his potential leadership. A young man who enters the army knows that a general's salary is less than magnificent as compared with that of the president of Ford Motor Company, but his decisions as a commander of the army affect the lives and destinies of many thousands of men. A civil servant can rise to become a diplomat whose actions can mean war or peace or a treaty favorable to his nation.

Yet scholars can—and have—influenced the world mightily, and thus the young professor can dream of that seminal work that will lend new insight into the world. Or that he will be Plato to another Aristotle, that some student whose mind he helps shape will be a world leader. Or even that his next article or book will cause men to think a little differently.

How quickly, however, the young scholar, if he be in that three-quarters of the specie that never publishes and only rarely teaches, realizes that his life is severely rounded about by his own limitations of laziness and ignorance. Still he dreams of writing, but never does; still he dreams of teaching, but reads old lecture notes.

He can do all these things and still fool himself about his worth because at the end of the year there is no way to tally his books with any accuracy. A businessman makes decisions and money is invested; merchandise is bought or plants are erected. And at the end of the year his books can be balanced and audited. Then, as plain as day, anyone can tell whether his decisions have earned money or lost money. But the scholar . . . No one can tell about him. There is no way to balance his books or audit his accounts. Has he taught well or poorly? How much have his students really learned? If he has written something, was it really a contribution to knowledge? No one knows. In fact, professors prefer it this way, saying that only someone within his own very limited field of competence can judge his contribution.

Yet at any given university, there usually is only one scholar in any given field. Let's face it, how many universities want two specialists on the poetry of Percy Bysshe Shelly! Or Oriental philosophies? Or most of the other narrow and specialized fields we carve out for ourselves to make certain no one else knows what we are doing. It is easy to be the frog of authority when you are the only one in your pond.

And we fight to see that no one comes in from the outside to judge us, claiming that the man in our narrow field from the next university will only criticize us out of jealousy or school rivalry. We are the only ones capable of judging our own performance, we claim, which is like saying that only General Motors is capable of telling us whether or not a Chevrolet is good or bad.

Locked in, therefore, by our inability to gain fortune or influence the world, scholars have only one dream left—fast promotion to full professor and huge pay raises to bring us to that top of the economic ladder within our chosen profession. Just as fast as possible the young assistant professor wants $25,000 a year and a tenured full professorship.

All too often in the past these have come within a relatively short span. Ten years or so has done it for most. Five years as an assistant professor and four or five years as an associate and there you have it—the young man has reached the highest he can ever aspire to without going into administrative work. If he is thirty when he gets his first job, that puts him at the top of his profession by the time he is forty, if not before. Then what? He still has twenty-five years or so before retirement. What is he supposed to do in the next quarter-century? The answer that comes to mind is "nothing," and that, unfortunately, is what too many of them do.

I have watched this process over many years and have noticed that somewhere between forty-five and fifty-five most professors finally make their compromise with life. Most finally admit that they are not going to write that great book or be that dazzling classroom performer that each secretly has dreamed of doing or being. I suspect the same thing goes on in the business world; most people in the corporate world about this age finally realize they are not going to be president of the company, just as most county court house politicians that age decide they will not become president of the United States. I think this is when men really begin to age—when they realize the futility of their dreams and then cease to dream. When a man ceases to dream, he is dead. Oh, he may not have laid down yet, but he is dead.

For the few professors who do continue to work and to dream, there is always the frustration of limited horizons. So what if he does a great job in the classroom? So what if he writes a book of moderate success or an article that is published in the top journal in his field? He will be paid about the same as the next fellow who does neither good teaching nor good writing. In short, he faces the futility of limited horizons.

A friend and I were discussing this situation one day. Inasmuch as he and I naturally felt ourselves to be part of the good-guy gang that is underpaid, overworked, and underrecognized, he commented to me, "You know, we're a couple of fools. If we had gone into business and had worked as hard as we do here, we'd be millionaires."

Perhaps, just perhaps. But then we don't really know whether or not we would be members of the good-guy team there. College professing has never tested us sufficiently for us really to judge our ability. The level of competition here is awfully low.

Do I, therefore, recommend that people should continue to dream? No! The good ones will dream regardless, and my recommendation might only lead to frustration for some dullard.

Yet I do believe that part of the real purpose of education ought to be teaching young people that, on occasion, a bird in the bush is worth two in the hand.

TOO MUCH, TOO SOON

Years ago, as I recall, there was a book by an heiress on the subject of too much, too soon. The concept was the "poor little rich girl" suffering from an overabundance of money. I have noticed that the same principle works in higher education, but in a different way. For example, I have seen a few hotshots come out of graduate school and get their dissertations accepted for publication by a New York house; these appear to great reviews in the newspapers and the academic journals, and some even win high prizes. Then the young professor freezes up, afraid to try anything again for fear of not being able to match what was in his first effort. One of my acquaintances, working in the same field of history in which I labor, graduated from an Ivy League school, had his dissertation published, and won the Pulitzer Prize for it. Since then he has not ventured into print again (except to pull one chapter out of that work and see it through the press as a monograph). Today he is employed at a major state university and spends his time writing harsh reviews of the books published by anyone who writes on the field of history he considers his own. But he writes nothing himself, a classic example of too much, too soon.

One friend to whom almost the same thing happened told me all I needed to know about the process. I had asked him if he was afraid that anything else he did might be compared unfavorably with his first effort and then everyone would think the prize-winning book was just a fluke. "You're so right," he said. "It causes you to freeze up."

If, on the other hand, this friend had written half a dozen books previously and had been cut by the reviewers, he would have been able to put the prize in perspective and continue to work. Anyone who has written much knows that those of his books which sell well and even win prizes are no better—if as good—as those which did not. Sometimes the prize-winning effort is the result of good timing (writing on Indians when the subject is hot, for example) or that the committee that selected the prize winners happened to contain a friend or two. But rarely will the book that won a prize be considered by an author to be his best effort.

If, therefore, the author gets knocked a few times on books he considers good, he can stand success and continue to work. There is a lot to be said, in the vernacular of the acting profession, for "paying your dues."

This brings me to today's college students. Few of them have paid their dues in life as yet, and some of them constitute a classic case of too much, too soon. When they arrive at college, almost everything they have ever had in life has been given to them. Overly generous parents have given them their cars, their wardrobes, their stereo sets, their pocket money. I recall walking across the campus once with a fellow student, one who was somewhat cynical. We observed a new Cadillac convertible in the student parking lot, which prompted the cynic to comment, "I'll bet that fellow had to work pretty hard last summer to earn enough money to buy that car and still have enough left to go to school this fall."

Which reminds me of another story. I was talking once with a fellow in campus security, one who was in charge of registering student automobiles. He told me that during the current semester there were seven students on campus who had registered brand-new Cadillacs—and that five of the seven had misspelled the word "Cadillac" on the application for a student parking permit. I suppose the moral of the story, if there was one, is that the student fortunate enough to pick a wealthy father doesn't need to be overly concerned with learning to spell.

Not only have many of our students had everything given to them, but also they have done almost everything by the time they get to college, and as a result are bored. Not too many years ago, students came to college and were thrilled to death at the thought of a formal dance, of the rah-rah of high-pressure

63

athletics, of the color of pep rallies and cheer leaders, of dating. But this is the generation that got full football equipment for elementary games—complete with cheer leaders urging the crowd to yell and the players to win. This is the generation whose parents pushed them to begin dating at twelve or thirteen (and when I was teaching seventh grade, I saw mothers willing to drive a daughter and her date to the movie and pick them up afterward—chauffeured dates for those too young to drive). These kids began going to formal dances complete with corsages when they were in junior high school, and they had the family car—if not their own—when they turned sixteen.

There even were beauty contests to pick homecoming queens both in junior high and high school. And, as an aside, I note here my objection to beauty contests. The bad part is that they distort values, giving some people the idea that looks are all that count in life. Not hard work, not personality, not kindness. Just good looks. I have a friend, a photographer, who says that he has known several beauty contest winners and that someday he is going to write a book on the subject entitled, *Don't Envy Them*.

Moreover, too many of the present generation of college students have had lives that were overly organized by well-intentioned parents. They have run from ballet lessons to scouts to piano, judo, swimming, horseback-riding, tennis, and golf lessons, all complete with costumes and equipment. They never have had the time which all youngsters should have to watch the grass grow and see the clouds change shape—and learn to dream big dreams. If ever youngsters are to develop an imagination, it is when they are in their pre- and early teens. But today they are bored. "There's nothing to do," they shout when their closets are full of games and toys and sports equipment and clothes and costumes. Yet, if you watch a small child, he often will have more fun with the carton in which a toy comes than with the toy itself; what I am saying is that the child who is forced to develop his imagination is far better off than the one given everything. (Those of us raised with radio, I believe, were more fortunate that the current generation raised with television; we had to imagine what the Lone Ranger or Superman or Jack Armstrong looked like—and it was far better than anything that television has done.)

Sadly, these youngsters have never had to learn to want something badly. Let too many of them say they want something, and their parents will give it to them (even if it means going into debt). Yet one of the real pleasures of life is looking forward to having something; in fact, looking forward to having something often is more fun that actually possessing it. I recall a fellow in the Marine Corps telling me about a woman he knew in Chicago whose major goal was to own a new Cadillac. For fourteen years she saved from her salary as a scrub woman, putting away a few dollars each week in order to accumulate enough to buy the car. When she finally got it, he asked her how she liked it. She replied, "Having it is not as much fun as looking forward to it was." This is one reason the rich are bored—they never have had the pleasure of looking forward to owning something.

Moreover, these youngsters with everything given them have never known the pride of earning something for themselves. The twelve-year-old works hard, saves his money, and buys his own bicycle has the pleasure of looking forward to owning the machine—and, when he gets it, the self-pride of accomplishment. Yet today we make it almost impossible for a youngster to gain this type of pride and sense of accomplishment. We have a number of laws on the books that make it almost impossible for anyone under sixteen to get a job. The intent of these laws, to prevent the abuse of children, is admirable, but what is the young boy or girl not yet sixteen and therefore old enough to suit the law, to do if he wants to earn money?

Nor are they able to learn the joy of work. Some French philosopher of the 18th century—and I forget his name—commented that the true joy of life is derived not from accomplishment but from work itself. A sort of "the medium is the message" kind of thought. The fun of writing a book, for me, is in the writing itself, not in seeing the thing done and mailing it off. Too few youngsters today have learned that work is an end in itself and that it is rewarding. Perhaps to this generation of pleasure-seekers the Madison Avenue hucksters should mount a campaign saying "Work Is Fun."

Out of all of this we have produced a generation accustomed to instant gratification, one unable to work, one without the pride of accomplishment, one that by the time it reaches eighteen years of age has tried everything and done everything. Then they come to college—only to find it is no big deal to a generation that had sororities and fraternities in high school. Little wonder that they expect everything to be given to them without work and without waiting: grades, diplomas, jobs. When at last they get into the real world, they learn that these things do not come automatically, and they feel cheated. Life somehow has done them wrong—and the system should be changed! All this stems from that most human of motives, wanting our children to have it better than we did. If, in truth, most parents want their children to have a good life, then they should teach their children the pleasure of work, allow them time to dream, not give them everything so that they will learn to want, and, above all, allow them to develop that sense of pride and self-worth that comes from accomplishment.

To many people this philosophy will sound wrong. It will, in their minds, label me a hopeless old fogey. Yet the great trage-dy to me is that some of these youngsters who have had life easy do not get out in the real world and learn any different. Instead they become professors and stay insulated. It is this crowd that does not believe in work or know the pride of accomplishment that should not be allowed to teach at any level. Rather, they should have to string barbed wire for a while. I have found this is a real builder of character. I am reminded of that every time I see students wearing bib-overalls or blue work shirts; those of us who grew up in the things could not wait to get out of them—just as these people would be if they had to earn their bib-overalls and blue work shirts by the sweat of their brows.

STUDENTS AND WRITING

When I was in graduate school, we had as a member of the faculty a man who personified the absent-minded professor. I recall talking with one fellow who told me that eighteen months after he graduated and had been at work for a certain company, a letter of recommendation arrived about him. His mystified employer asked about the letter; was he looking around? Had the letter come there by mistake? He checked into the matter only to learn that this absent-minded professor had been asked for a letter about him, and laid the request aside, and then had found it eighteen months later—and had belatedly written the letter.

The head of the department and I were talking about that particular professor one day, and he told me, "I'd heard all the stories about his absent-mindedness, so I decided to check it out. I was told that if I met him going across campus and talked to him, that he would forget where he was going. So the other day I saw him and we began to talk. As we talked, I gradually eased him around to face the opposite direction he had been going. And, sure enough, when we finished, he set out walking briskly in the direction he was facing—which was where he was coming from when we met."

Yes, that old professor was always good for a laugh. But he also was one of the sharpest men I ever have met—in some ways. One day he got to telling me about a master's candidate whose committee he was sitting on. The student was taking a master of education degree with a history minor, and he had written his thesis. The absent-minded professor told me—truthfully—that he always checked every source citied in every thesis he read, and that in this case he could not find a single one of the sources listed. Yet, when he protested this fact to the professor of education directing the work, the fellow had reacted first with indignation and then with anger, finally going to the graduate dean and asking that the absent-minded history professor be removed from the committee. Another man was appointed, the thesis was duly accepted, and the degree was awarded.

It happened in this case that I knew the student in question, and I asked him about the incident. He laughed a long time before he could talk. "No wonder he couldn't find my sources," the student cackled. "I wrote the thesis and then I had a friend make up all the footnotes. I knew those professors in education would never check."

I tell this story to show that almost two decades ago we had students trying to avoid the hard work involved in writing. That particular student was one of the imaginative ones; at least he wrote his own thesis. There were those, then as now, who lacked the imagination and who simply copied the entire thing from one book or another. That is a practice known as plagiarism. The most flagrant cases I ever saw both happened to the same professor, a friend of mine. In one case he had a graduate student turn in a dissertation that in its introduction sounded very familiar—and no wonder, for the introduction was copied from an extremely well-known work written by the professor under whom my friend had studied. The doctoral candidate's excuse was, "But I didn't know that was plagiarism."

In the other case, my friend had a student turn in a book review which also sounded familiar. In checking, he found that the review had been copied from a learned journal—and the original review in that learned journal had been written by the professor's own wife. That graduate student should have been flunked more on the grounds of stupidity than for plagiarism.

Yes, there always was cheating on college papers and theses and dissertations. Undergraduate students, when assigned a term paper, would hustle around and try to find someone who had done a term paper for another professor on the same subject, then would copy that and turn it in as their own. Fraternities and sororities kept files of all the term papers written over the years by their members. And athletes were given help by "tutors" who, in effect, wrote their papers for them so they could stay eligible.

But today a black market enterprise system has made it possible for the student to go through without the risk of plagiarism. Just as math students have pocket electronic computers available to do the hard part of their work, so the student faced with writing has help available to do his dirty work. There now are companies that for a fee will do research for you. All you have to do, besides paying them, is send them your subject and they will send you a bibliography on the subject. In fact, I recall an encyclopedia salesman who came by my house one evening to sell me his wares (interestingly I had done an article in that set, but after watching the sales pitch he made I never told anyone about it); part of his spiel was to tell me that with the encyclopedias came the right to have their staff do research for me. I would receive a set of coupons, and when I needed something I was to tear off a coupon and enclose it with my request for instant research. Part of his sales pitch was aimed at parents with children in college or even high school, and the implication clearly made was that I did not want my children to do well if I did not make this service available to them.

However, this encyclopedia company was behind the times, for now there are companies openly advertising in campus newspapers that for a fee they will supply term papers already written—with a bibliography included at the end. The fee for this service is based on how original you want the paper. If you are willing to turn in a paper sold to a student at some other school, the cost is less than if you want something original. There has been quite a furor in higher education in recent months about this "business" and what the reaction ought to be.

Yet all of this is as nothing compared to the question of what to do about the companies that will write a thesis or dissertation for the graduate student. (Here let me note that one of the major philosophical bases of graduate education is that the student has to demonstrate his capacity to do original research and writing; if, therefore, he buys his dissertation ready-written, he has avoided a major part of his education.) The cost for this service depends on the length thesis or dissertation the student wants, as well as on the difficulty of the subject, but a good average now is $1,500 for a thesis and $4,500 for a dissertation. Back when I was in graduate school, there were a few freelance types on campus who would write a thesis for you for $500 or a dissertation for $2,000; in fact, I knew one student who liked to write and who did it easily who put himself through graduate school this way. But that was by word-of-mouth advertising from his satisfied customers—and on a very small scale. Now it is done by companies whose sole product is ready-written term papers, theses, and dissertations, and they are advertising openly across the country.

Ironically, these companies are headquartered in and around the major universities of the nation (several, for example, are in the Boston area). These are schools that in the past have posed before the country as the major sites for graduate study, places that turn out quality students. Now we learn that they also are centers for perverting the very excellence that they claim to have possessed all these years.

No easy solution to this problem has been found as yet. A professor with thirty or forty students in a class cannot tell who did the work themselves and who bought it ready made (I refrain from pointing out that many professors are not competent to judge the originality of their term papers anyway). Some college teachers have called for federal legislation to end this blight on higher education; others are envious of the financial success of the companies, while yet another part of the profession wants to keep the whole thing quiet. Those in the latter category, no doubt, include some who purchased their own theses and dissertations already written.

The result of this new black market system is that, just as we have a generation unable to balance their checkbooks and do simple sums in arithmetic, so also we have a generation unable to research and write—and, all too often, professors who, after purchasing their own term papers and scholarly product, are unable to teach their students how to do the work themselves.

All of them, students and professors, need to learn the maxim known to every mature scholar: "Plagiarism is stealing (or buying) from one source; research is stealing from several sources."

PLACING GRADUATES FROM COLLEGE

The sudden closing of the job market for college graduates which came about 1970 or 1971 created real shock waves on college campuses across the United States—and even has caused some hard thinking among professors about the purpose of higher education. Prior to that point we expected our graduates to find jobs easily. In fact, employers were expected to line up and bid for the services of these people, and to offer starting salaries ever increasing in size. Each year the placement service on each campus put out a notice about how starting salaries for college graduates were 6, 8, even 10 percent higher than last year, and how the average graduate had an offer of four of five jobs.

High school teachers used these figures to point out to their students the value of high education. The person with an eighth-grade education could expect to make an average of $250,000 in a lifetime, while the average high school graduate could expect some $325,000 in a lifetime. And the college graduate could expect a handsome $425,000 or so in a lifetime. Using these figures, it was easy for high school teachers to say to their students, "Study hard here, get into college, graduate, and have an extra $100,000 in your lifetime." I've quoted those figures myself when I was in the public schools to try to say—as do other teachers—you had better work for me or I'll flunk you and you won't get into college. It was a handy stick with which to beat restless students into line.

Suddenly, however, the employers were not at the college placement offices. Not offering higher wages. Not offering the same wages as last year. There were not four or five job offers. For many graduates there was no offer at all. Especially in areas like public school teaching, the liberal arts, and the humanities. The only place the job market has held fairly firm is in the hard sciences, engineering, agriculture, and various phases of business administration (especially accounting; in fact, graduates with degrees in accounting have been getting the highest starting salaries of any discipline for the last two or

71

three years).

This sudden, strange twist has forced many college instructors to think about the real purpose of a college education, especially those professors in the liberal arts, the humanities, and the social sciences. These have been the very people who have looked with contempt at the scientists, the engineers, the business majors, and students in agriculture. "Those are not really college subjects," the humanists have said with disdain. "They are really *technicians*." They emphasized the word technicians to imply that it really was almost dirty.

Their idea seems to have been that anything practical, anything that involved working with one's hands as well as one's head, was not true education. This belief no doubt stems from the historic function of a university. Back in the Middle Ages, when universities as we know them were developing, institutions of higher learning had only one purpose: to educate society's leaders. In those days the leaders were the nobility, the clergy, and professions such as doctors and lawyers. They were given a standard education in many ways: all studied Latin, philosophy, theology, history—in short, the liberal arts. These graduates of universities were expected never to work with their hands, certainly not at anything practical. In fact, they were trained to do nothing, *but with style*.

Today those professors in the liberal arts, the humanities, and the social studies still believe that the only subjects that really constitute an education are foreign languages, philosophy, theology, and history—along with disciplines that have branched away from these traditional ones (such as sociology, psychology, geography, political science, etc.). Few of these are really practical. Graduates in those areas cannot build a bridge or grow a crop or mix chemicals or drill an oil well, but they could think lofty thoughts and discuss great literature and appreciate "culture."

And because of the economic good times that prevailed until recently, all college graduates could get jobs. The humanistic types, failing all else, could always get employed as teachers or become bureaucrats at some level of government. Since their graduates did get work, those professors in the liberal arts continued to look down their noses at all courses in the practical disciplines. They pleaded that all university graduates, to be educated, had to be exposed to courses in the liberal arts and got rules passed to force budding engineers, scientists, and farmers to take English, philosophy, history, political science, and the humanities—but screamed loudly when their own students were forced to take a little science and math.

Yet there always have been high school graduates who wanted to learn a skill without having to take these "humanistic studies." They learned to hate those subjects in high school from teachers trained in those disciplines. To avoid the same experience in college, increasing numbers of students have been going to vocational-technical schools—and there has been a phenomenal growth in vo-tech schools across the land. There students receive a practical education in a short period of time, learning a skill that will gain them lasting employment.

I suspect that most professors in the liberal arts and humanities would not have grown concerned about their graduates failing to get jobs, that they would continue to feel that their subjects constitute the only true "education," but the declining number of jobs for college graduates has been matched by declining enrollments in college. This has awakened the humanists in a hurry, for declining enrollments just might result in some of them being fired. Without students to teach, some of them might no longer be hired to teach, and then they would have to go out in the hard, cold, cruel world and make a living by working—even with their hands and backs and muscles and sweat. It is amazing how practical some of these professors become when confronted with this thought.

Suddenly "employability" as a goal of higher education no longer is such a dirty thought to the humanists. Somehow they are willing to admit that engineers just might be educated, that it might require some intelligence to become a farmer, that accounting has legitimacy on the college campus. They admit this because all these people have to take a few courses in the liberal arts, and that is the only way professors in these areas can stay in business. The job recession has brought a dramatic reduction in the number of history majors; the surplus of teachers has caused falling enrollments in colleges of education; the waning of the hippie movement has caused sociology to lose some of its glamor as a "social action" field of endeavor.

When it comes to a choice between admitting the legitimacy of practical disciplines as higher education as opposed to the purity of the liberal arts (and that means having a job and being able to eat without working), the humanists suddenly are very concerned with the employability of our graduates.

THE IDENTITY CRISIS

Almost every time I drive to the edge of town I see them standing beside the road, young people hitchhiking here and there, guitars strapped across their backs, sleeping bags laying on the ground—their only accomplishment seemingly the ability to grow hair. I have often wondered what these people are doing, but when I ask them about their goals they tell me they are in search of "who they are." I once knew a family whose son set out for Canada and other exotic points, searching for his identity. He was gone a couple of years, but eventually returned a little shaggier about the ears and the ring around his collar a little blacker—and still had not discovered who he was.

However, I have noted one thing about these people. They may be suffering an identity crisis, but they do seem to know something about the climate. I see them in Colorado in the summer and in Arizona during the winter. Apparently they have the same mentality as the swallows of Capistrano—they fly south in the winter and north in the summer; one can predict the seasons by their migrations.

These kids sometimes are urged forward in this quest for identity by professors telling them to "find truth in yourself." Somehow it seems to me that travel and introspection are not necessary companions. And happiness is something that comes from within, not from the area of the country you happen to be in. On the score of happiness I have noticed over the years that most people follow the words "I will be happy" with the word "when." "I will be happy when I graduate from high school." "I will be happy when I get out of the service." "I will be happy when I get out of college." "I will be happy when I get married." When the children are born. When the children are grown. When I retire.

The next thing you know, people like that are dead—and still they never have been happy.

Happiness, which equates in large measure with being secure in your knowledge of yourself (knowing your identity—or, as the kids now say, "getting it all together"), does not depend on your location or where you now stand on the road of life. Rather, it comes from within and is a "here and now" kind of thing. Moreover, happiness is not directly tied to your bank account, although my daddy used to say, "Whether you're rich or poor, it's nice to have money."

The thing about those professors who urge the kids to get out and find themselves is that they preach against materialism. They tell their students that happiness is not to be found in material possessions, and that the young would do well to turn their back on the quest for wealth. Yet these same professors would consider life not worth living if they did not have their air conditioned offices and cars, their double-knit suits, and their credit cards. In short, it is so easy for them to disdain materialism while enjoying all the things provided by their tenure and the taxpayers of the state. Most of these academic antimaterialists would scream to high heaven if they had to do without clean sheets for only a day or two.

Yet every spring these misguided young people set out on their quests for identity, their heads turned by the preachings of professors much as Don Quixote had his head turned by reading too many romantic novels and set out to joust windmills. The kids set out saying they do not want or need material things, but they live on checks from home while they search for themselves. I heard one old farmer say that if one of his kids ever set out on such a quest he would "break his plate." By this he meant that the child no longer would have a place set for him at the dinner table, or, in other words, that if the child were old enough to set out trying to find himself then he was old enough to make his own living while he was searching.

The sad part of all this is that anyone who lived through the Great Depression could easily tell these young people who they are: let them get hungry enough, either because they cannot steal something or else because the check from home fails to arrive, and they will learn that they are a set of teeth and a stomach. Most of the uneducated and deprived people of the world know this hard fact without benefit of philosophers and higher education.

Yet I am not really down on the kids for searching because I know that in a few years most of them will rejoin the world. Every generation has its 2 percent who drop out, the misfits and malcontents and ne'er-do-wells and permanent rebels. The other 98 percent soon will be carrying their attache cases and hurrying to make the 7:45 for the city. On one occasion I was talking with one of these rebels-without-a-cause and told him that in twenty years he would be straining for another rung up the corporate ladder and that his wife would be playing bridge in the country club. He shuddered visibly, thought a while, and concluded, "You're probably right."

Another, not quite so perceptive, assured me that his generation was made up of idealists and nonconformists. I noted the love-beads around his neck and said, "I'm glad to see you're wearing your hippie dog tags."

His eyes widened and then filled with rage. "What do you mean by saying I'm a conformist. I'm not! I'm not!" And he left my office.

Today the dirty look is beginning to disappear, and students are getting far more serious than they were five or even three years ago. I believe this is because the job market dried up somewhat, and they are beginning to realize what those without benefit of college knew all along: even if you don't know who you are, it's nice to eat regularly—and the world certainly looks a lot better on a full stomach.

THE NUMBERS GAME

In the good old days of higher education, the boom period of the 1960s, colleges and universities every autumn faced the problem of what to do with all the students wanting admission. Some of the really prestigious institutions openly advertised that five out of six who applied would be sent away to enroll at some lesser place. But most state schools took in everyone, for their budgets are tied very closely to enrollments; besides, as registrars told themselves, the professors can as easily lecture to seventy as to forty, so cram a few more chairs in every classroom and sign up all who walk in with money in their fists.

Professors reacted to these ever-increasing enrollments by trying—very deliberately and openly—to run off as many students as possible at the first of each semester. After all, the instructor's work load is far less if he has four classes with forty in each than if he has seventy in each; simple arithmetic told them this—that it takes less work to grade 160 sets of tests than it does to grade 280 sets of tests. So professors came to class on the first day of the semester, looking around at the horde of students, and almost gleefully proclaimed, "Next week half of you won't be here." Or "I always fail 40 percent of my classes."

I remember hearing students laugh at this practice. One told me, "Oh, he gave us the usual scare tactics and tried to run us off. But he didn't scare me. I'm staying in there."

Other professors would try to accomplish the same thing but in a more subtle way. They would go in on the first day of class and make an assignment for the following class that would take anyone three weeks to complete. This, of course, was an attempt to make the student believe the work load would be impossible in the course, and that he had best drop it.

Some professors used words, others work. Some did it gleefully, others with some sadness. But always the intent was the same: to run off a portion of the students.

Today, however, the situation has changed—and dramatically. Colleges and universities now are faced with enrollments that at best have stabilized at some level, and which at worst are falling. The baby boom of the early 1950s has ended, and declining birth rates during the rest of that decade now are reflected in the fewer freshmen arriving every fall. Moreover, the end of the draft, along with increasing junior college enrollments and the increasing number of young men and women who question the value and benefit to be gained from a college education, has contributed to the woes of colleges and universities.

Some schools actually have had to close as a result of declining enrollment. Principally these have been small, private institutions whose finances were marginal even during the good times. Many other institutions have had to retrench severely, especially those that at one time were teacher-training colleges; the major state universities have not been hurt as badly by this trend as have the old teachers' colleges—although today many of them do bear the name "university." The president of one of these former teacher-training schools, now labeled a university, told me, "I've built my last dormitory." And today many dorms do stand partially or fully empty because too few students are enrolling.

As a result of these diminishing enrollments, some institutions have had to let some faculty go, even tenured members of the faculty (see the chapter on firing), while those who still have a job now are playing what increasingly is known as the numbers game. Professors who once bragged at the number of students they ran off at the start of each semester or the outrageous number of students they failed at the end of each semester—all of which they naturally justified on the basis of their "high standards"—now worship at the shrine of numbers. They brag about the number of students taking their courses, and they brag about the few who fail. I know of a few professors whose grades once averaged about a C minus (or even, as one prof once said to me about the grade a student made in his class, "He got a C minus with a droop on the end of the minus") and who shouted loudly on every occasion about their high standards, who now give grades that average a B plus or an A minus.

Somehow, having high standards does not seem as important as having a job next fall.

Moreover, the numbers game has been complicated by the increasing sophistication of the student body. Youngsters coming to college today will not put up with the bullying that their parents did. A professor today who threatens to fail a quarter of his class or who assigns an unreasonable amount of work quickly will find himself on the dean's carpet, for deans are even more fully aware of the need to get students than are the instructors. Or, if not the dean's carpet, he will find himself facing an empty classroom by the second week of school; students will simply drop such a course. If it is a required course, one they must have to graduate, they will try to take it under someone else. But if that professor is the only one teaching it, they will lobby to have the rules for graduation changed—and there is increasing sophistication on the part of students about campus politics—or else they will go to the department head, the dean, the vice president for academic affairs, even to the president to make known their displeasure at the professor who is unreasonably hard.

Moreover, students increasingly are pushing for a no-failure policy. They want to change the system through various means to insure that none of them receives an F in a course. At some institutions this movement has brought a policy of allowing any student to declare a semester of "academic bankruptcy"—that is, to remove from a student's transcript all records of any given semester in which he does badly. The reasoning here is that some students occasionally have a semester in which they do very badly in everything; perhaps a parent died or the parents divorced or there was an unhappy affair of the heart, but for whatever reason the student simply failed everything. So he wants that entire semester's results removed from his transcript. And some universities do allow for this.

Other universities have taken a different approach. They allow the student to drop any course in which his grade is not pleasing. Even to drop it right up to the week of finals. This means the student goes to class all semester (or fails to go to class), takes the tests, does everything, but if at any time he decides his grades are not good, he can pick up a card at the registrar's office and have it signed by the professor; then, on his transcript all that shows is a W—which means he withdrew from the course. And a W does not count on his grade point average.

Finally, students are demanding a better deal from professors through their willingness to sue. Almost every institution now has what generally is called an "academic appeals board" to which the student can appeal any grade he thinks is unfair. At the meetings of this board, the student presents his side of the case and the professor defends his practices; then the members of the academic appeals board (which usually does include some members who are students) vote on the case. And these do change grades regularly.

And some students do not stop there. They are going into the regular civil courts to sue universities. One of the things which slowed down the professors who were supporting the radicals during the protests against the Vietnam War a few years ago was law suits by students against the universities that closed; the student could sue that he had paid his tuition for classes, that these classes had not met, and that the university—even the individual professor—was liable.

Actually, however, the students do not have to push most professors hard these days to get good grades. The truth is, standards have been drastically lowered by instructors who once talked endlessly about their standards, for the threat of colleges having to let go some faculty members has scared almost everyone.

And the stabilizing or declining enrollments have made colleges and universities far more sophisticated in recruiting. In many states the use of funds for recruiting is prohibited. In those places school administrators get around that rule by using state money for "advising"—which consists mainly of advising the students to come to the school "advising" them. Most universities are creating departments of "high school and junior college relations." The purpose, of course, is to persuade as many of these people as possible to come to them.

And universities are getting very sophisticated in their

recruitment practices. They are hiring public relations experts to do brochures, even sixteen millimeter sight-and-sound films, that make life at good old Siwash University look like one long round of fun. Universities and colleges are adopting the techniques of the toothpaste and cigarette salesmen, implying that going to their school will make you more attractive to the opposite sex, guarantee you a high income, and give you a life free from all worries and cares.

Some students believe all this, and they come to the campus in the fall—only to discover that everything promised in the brochures and films is not true. This naturally makes them somewhat unhappy, which in turn leads to yet more pressure to change the system. Make grades easier. End all dorm hours. Force the professors to do a better job in the classroom. In short, the whole thing I have been describing in this chapter goes round in a circle.

III
Miscellaneous Opinions

CLOSED MINDS

Once when I was in graduate school, a friend (one of the two to whom this book is dedicated) asked me something or other, to which I replied that I had no opinion on the subject. "Nonsense," he responded, "you're never at a loss for an opinion." I have always been grateful to him for this comment—if for no other reason that it now serves as the title for this book. Moreover, in the fairyland of college professing, it has served as a warning against developing a closed mind.

And the danger is a very real one amongst my professorial colleagues. There is something about this business that makes us think we know the answer to almost every question. I think the same thing happens to bureaucrats in the federal government. I recall sitting at one meeting in which a fellow was explaining the beauties of working for the civil service. When he finished his presentation, someone in the audience asked a question.

With a straight face, the bureaucrat replied, "It is difficult for me to answer your question because I don't know the answer. But. . . ." And he proceeded to talk for ten minutes.

Most of the people who reacted very negatively to *This Beats Working for a Living* were those who apparently see the professorhood as a kind of priesthood, and to attack them is to attack God himself. By this I mean they reacted with a kind of shocked disbelief that I would speak heresy. We all, at one time or another, have known what, for want of a better description, could be classified as religious fanatics. These are people who are quick to tell you exactly what God wants in any given situation (I have noted how surprising it is that God always seems to want exactly what these people want). Too many professors speak in the same way—as if they have a private telephone line to Heaven and every morning have a little chat with the Man himself.

I see it on the evening news where some professor of literature says exploding a nuclear bomb in the Aleutian Islands will cause a prolonged series of earthquakes. He says it with such conviction that you are certain he knows exactly what he is talking about. And then, somehow, when the bomb is exploded, the earthquake fails to arrive on schedule. I can almost imagine the fellow being dissappointed that the calamity did not take place.

Or we see some psychology professor (with a beard, naturally) telling us that to build a pipeline across Alaska will have all kinds of dire consequences, from the death of the entire moose population to bad breath for the Eskimos. Then, when the energy crisis arrives at last, his only answer is to swear that it is a conspiracy on the part of the oil company executives to raise the price of gasoline. Somehow these fellows never see any connection between events and consequences.

Yes, I live in a world where the closed mind is regarded as a virtue—yet where lip service is paid constantly to "being open to the truth." How then can I satirize the breed if I myself am never at a loss for an opinion? Because I reserve the right to change my opinions. And, in fact, I do find them changing as age turns the color of my hair (and I'd much rather it turn gray than turn loose).

To give one example of my changing opinions, for example,

when I was sixteen I believed that anyone who had the price in his pocket should be allowed to buy beer. Then when I got to be eighteen, I thought, "Well, they shouldn't let those kids buy beer, but anyone old enough to join the service should be allowed to buy beer." Then I got to be twenty-one, and I decided those legislators knew what they were doing; anyone under age twenty-one should not be allowed to drink. When I got past thirty, I began to believe that the legal age for drinking should be raised at least to twenty-five. Now, with still more years added to my score, I rarely drink at all and wonder seriously at anyone who does.

The same with the voting age. During this recent debate to lower the thing to eighteen, I totally believed that it should be moved only in the upward direction, not downward. Each year I become more certain of it.

And on the subject of when a person gains wisdom, well, at age sixteen I knew it all. Now I have arrived at the point where I believe at least four decades, if not more, are necessary: that is, I think a few gray hairs indicate the onset of maturity just as a quivering voice indicates the onset of puberty.

I am never at a loss for an opinion, but from year to year those do change somewhat.

CLOTHES

"Clothes make the man" says a widely repeated cliché. I guess that is right, for I have seen few of them walking around naked. Heaven knows I don't want to see most people walking around that way. The current fashions have approached about as near to nudity as possible, even more than most people want. You look in the summer at those people wearing very little—and you will find that only 1 or 2 percent of such people are attractive. The truth is that most people look best when well dressed. Here I recall a course I once had in ancient history wherein the prof was telling about one of the Greek city states wherein total nudity became fashionable; a couple of years later the rulers of the city had to pass a decree forbidding nudity because the birth rate had plummeted so drastically.

In the academic world, as in business, there are some people who make a reputation for dressing to the hilt. They are flashy, debonair, stylish. These are the kind who now arrive wearing white shoes and white belt, double-knit trousers of an outlandish hue, a peach-colored shirt, and a purple or red sports coat. They are the ones who arrive at some social function in a blue tuxedo with ruffled shirt. You know the kind I mean—the ones who wear a flashy diamond ring on their little fingers. These people remind me of a story I once heard about a professor who came to class the first day and read off the class roll. The second day he arrived and overwhelmed the class by calling the roll from memory. "I was really impressed," one student told me, "until I found out that this was his entire bag of tricks." The same is often true of these flashy dressers; that is their entire bag of tricks. Interestingly I have observed that the ones who rely on a stylish wardrobe for advancement usually are the ones seeking some administrative post. They rarely learn that the good administrator has more going for him than a big wardrobe.

Many scholars really believe that administrators must be dressed to the hilt at all times and that dressing like one will result in promotion. And the reverse happens. At a convention once I was talking with a friend about a mutual acquaintance who had just been promoted to assistant dean. My friend commented, "It must be awfully cold over there in the administration building."

"How do you figure that?" I asked.

"Well, when that old boy was just a member of the department, he always went around in shirt sleeves, his tie hanging loose. He rarely ever wore a coat. But now, when I see him, he always has his tie pulled up tight around his neck, and he's always wearing a coat buttoned up. I just figure it's cold over there in the administration building."

The more I reflect on that observation, the more I realize all administration buildings must be cold at every college and university—and in every business and in government.

THIEVERY

We live in the age of the rip-off. That is a phrase current among college students and the hip types which means to steal. There even was a book a couple of years ago, by a fellow setting himself up as a guru for the young militants, entitled *Steal This Book*.

My advice on this score is that if you must steal, do it big. Don't try for a few paltry dollars. Wait until you can get a least half a million, but even more than that is best. If you steal big, you can hire a good lawyer. If you steal enough, then you will be rich enough to hire F. Lee Bailey or someone of that caliber to defend you. Also, remember that you will likely go to jail longer for writing a hot check for fifty dollars than for stealing five million dollars. I recall reading in the paper over the years about this chap or that one who lifted ten or twenty million through stock swindles or fraud or embezzlement and then got a one or two year sentence.

The trouble with academicians is that they steal small. They send personal mail out on departmental stationery and using the department's stamps. They take home a ream of typing paper for which they do not pay. They lift pencils and ball point pens and paper clips, and they cheat on their mileage for using personal cars; they cut classes short and they do not update their lectures, which is a form of stealing in that they want full salaries; they use campus Xerox machines to duplicate personal materials; they even fill their coffee cups from the department's coffee machine and fail to put their nickels in the box. They also steal their lectures, just as many of them steal their ideas from the work of others in their fields. Yes, they steal, but stupidly. However, I guess if they had the vision to steal really big, they would also have the vision not to have entered this profession.

THE VALUE OF CONSISTENT MEDIOCRITY

If you are driving down the highway at lunchtime and are in a part of the country with which you are unfamiliar, you have the problem of where to get a decent meal. You see a sign proclaiming *EATS*—which has always struck my fancy as a funny name for a restaurant. However, such a sign leaves you in a quandary: will you find gourmet food, or will you get ptomaine poisoning? The truth is, you don't know. However, if you stop at the Colonel's fried chicken place, be it in the East or the West, North or South, you know exactly what you will get; it won't be a dining delight, but it will be digestable.

Or if you are driving down the road and sundown is approaching, you need to find a place to sleep, one about which your wife and kids will not complain as being beneath their dignity. You see a sign proclaiming *Dreamland Motel.* You feel fairly certain it will not be the Ritz, but which will it be: bedbugs or high class? There is no way to know unless you have stayed there before. However, you see a sign proclaiming one of the national chain motels, you can be assured that it means a relatively clean room at a relatively decent price.

As I view these two items, food and lodging, I conclude that the secret of success in modern America is guaranteeing consistent, uniform, dependable mediocrity. The weary or hungry traveler knows exactly what he will find, for it will be a duplicate of what he found at the last motel or restaurant in that chain. This is true whether he be in Bangor, Maine, or Capistrano, California, in Del Rio, Texas, or Juneau, Alaska. It never will be first class, but it will not be the bottom of the barrel.

For the young man seeking his fortune in this great, wide world, my advice would be to find some human need and fill it with consistent mediocrity. Unfortunately for the young Horatio Alger, the gasoline, food, and motel businesses already are glutted. I do know of one area where such an aspiring millionaire might find profits, and I herewith give the idea away. I really don't want to give it away free, so whoever reads this and get inspired I hope will remember me and cut me in for 1 percent of the gross. Or even just one-half of 1 percent of the gross.

The area I believe to be uncrowded and where consistent mediocrity would bring in millions is the lawn care field. I know that every summer, when I leave for my all-too-short vacation, I have the recurring problem of finding someone to care for my lawn, shrubbery, and trees. The average homeowner has a substantial investment in these things, the prices being what they are at the typical nursery these days. I recall two summers ago when I was about to leave I contracted with one of the local nurseries to care for my lawn. I returned two weeks later to find my grass yellowed and my trees wilting; only the fact that a kindly neighbor saw what was happening and watered my trees kept them from dying. When I complained to the nursery that had agreed to do the work, I was told that someone in the office must have misplaced its contract with me. Of course, I could have sued them, but that would not bring my plants back to life, nor would I have been able to make them pay without a substantial investment in lawyer's fees (and there probably is no profession in America which profits so much from consistent mediocrity; rarely have I gone to a lawyer for advice or help without, in the end, having to go to the statute books myself and tell him what I want done).

If some enterprising fellow would start a lawn care service in my town and keep good books on how much money is to be made, eventually he could franchise the service all across America. These lawn care centers would have all the business they wanted from people on vacation, from hospitals and apartment houses, from elderly people no longer able to care for their yards, from little old ladies who want beautiful yards but do not want to work, and from people who own two houses and cannot take care of both yards simultaneously. The number of clients for such a service would be long. And workers would be had easily; the bulk of such work comes in the summer when there are thousands of high school and college boys needing summer employment, some of them even willing to work in return for a salary. The investment in such a business would not be large: a few lawnmowers and some garden hose and sprinklers, a couple of pickup trucks, and perhaps a fertilizer spreader and hedge-trimmer.

Eventually a smart entrepreneur in charge of a national chain of lawn care centers could start selling his own line of lawnmowers (manufactured to his specifications), garden hose, fertilizer, insecticides, peat moss, tools, etc. The possibilities stagger the imagination. As I said earlier, I just hope that whoever jumps on this remembers me and pays me a small percentage of the gross—even just 1 percent.

Now, to transfer this concept to guaranteed consistent mediocrity to the academic world. There are many colleges and universities that attract students and maintain their standing through consistent mediocrity. They never innovate. They offer new courses and degrees only when these have proven themselves elsewhere. They maintain low standards. They hire faculty members who give an indication they will not rock the boat. And they admit almost anyone who applies: I know—and you probably do also—several schools that get a large portion of their enrollments by admitting students who have flunked out elsewhere or who have high school grades so low that they cannot get in anywhere else. I have heard such schools referred to as "retread universities." They take in those students who have had a blow-out elsewhere.

Speaking of this reminds me of one "university" located within fifty miles of two major schools. It attracts the students who cannot get into the two better institutions and those afraid to attempt the two more difficult ones. And it takes anyone who flunks out of the others; the only requirements for admission at this institution are to be breathing and to have money in a hot fist. The president of that institution retires next year—and I truly pity the poor fellow who follows him. If the new prexy attempts to raise standards, his enrollment will drop disastrously and he will lose his job because of complaints from local merchants and from alumni. And if he does not raise standards, the institution will never amount to anything. I guess the thing for him to do is to settle for consistent mediocrity in advance or else have a backup job.

And there are many professors—sad to say, the majority of them—who settle for consistent mediocrity. In this business it is remarkably easy to rise to the top. Inasmuch as most professors never publish, a man with an itch to get to the top only has to do a few articles and an occasional book to be in the top 10 percent. Inasmuch as most profs are wretched lecturers, all the ambitious fellow has to do is work moderately hard at this aspect of the profession to win teaching awards. However, to do these—write and work at teaching—is to invite criticism and even hatred. One of my acquaintances recently published a book and was astonished to find that it was torn to pieces by reviewers on the flimsiest of grounds. He told me, "What burns me up is that the reviewers did not hit me where there was legitimate ground for doing so. I know there were weak points in my book. But they didn't hit these. Instead they tried to get me for failing to include things they wanted in it or for missing a few Spanish accents."

I tried to console the fellow by pointing out that for the next few years these mediocre types will cut at him needlessly and pointlessly. They do it because he is working and trying to do better than a mediocre job. If he persists, however, he will find those same people will be coming up to him at conventions and saying they are his best friends, that they have always admired him, and that he is a great man. Anytime a man sticks his head above the crowd, he had better be prepared for the knife.

Mediocrity is not exclusive to the academic world. Auto mechanics, television repairmen, even major manufacturing concerns make a good living every year selling mediocre goods and services to the public. Thus colleges and universities should not be singled out for exclusive criticism on that score. However, some of it is deserved when it comes to higher education, for no professor or administrator worth his salt should work for anything less than excellence. If higher education is to be worth the time and money of the young, it should strive for excellence. And, God knows, the level of competition is such that just a little work will make a school stand out; a little striving will make for better than mediocrity.

Unfortunately, there are few schools or professors trying for more. We settle for chain motels and chain fried chicken or hamburgers and chain income tax preparers, so why not a chain of mediocre colleges? We could even start advertising these on television and set up a teletype reservation service. And when the public gets tired of the standard courses, we offer "extra crunchy" courses or a 19¢ reduction on the Big Mac if they also order french fries. A little more good thinking like this and I may apply to be president of that school next year!

A JOURNAL FOR REJECTED ACADEMIC ARTICLES

A friend and I once were discussing, over a cup of coffee, the sad fact that editors of scholarly journals reject articles on the flimsiest of reasons. We decided what we ought to do was to start a journal for rejected articles, one devoted to publishing nothing else.

"We'll insist that everyone of these be accompanied by at least three letters of rejection from standard journals," my friend exclaimed, warming to the thought.

"Yes," I said, "and we won't edit a bit. We'll run them exactly as they come in without a comma added or period changed. We won't paragraph or rewrite."

My friend liked that idea in that it meant we would not have to work. "In fact," he added, "let's not even read proof. We'll let the author do any of that he wants, but if he doesn't want to we won't do it ourselves."

We even came up with a title, *The Journal of Rejected History!*

Then we got around to a discussion of financing this academic wonder child. That did pose a problem inasmuch as neither of us could afford to underwrite the effort, nor could we think of any academic institution or organization that would put up the money. For a time we toyed with the idea of charging the authors, but we decided that if they couldn't sell the material anywhere else they wouldn't have the money to pay what are known as page charges (that is, charging the author so many dollars for each page his article runs in print).

In the end, however, the idea died not for want of financing but because we realized the journal would not sell. After all, who would want to buy our journal when he would not be able to tell a bit of difference between it and all the other academic journals being published and to which he probably already was subscribing?

THE DIRTY JOKE TEST OF CHARACTER

"Did you hear the one about the traveling salesman who...?"

Over the years I have watched people's reactions when dirty jokes are told, and I have observed that you can get a quick index to a man's character by his reactions. Here I am not advocating telling them in mixed company, but rather about what you can learn about colleagues with whom you regularly come into contact. Nor do I feel you should belt out a strong one when you meet a group of strangers. In fact, you can learn something about people by watching when they tell dirty jokes; there is a time and a place for them, and the man whom you can trust has an innate sense of timing and decency about these things.

However, when one is told, watch reactions. The fellow who turns up his nose in disgust and refuses to laugh or even stomps away in high moral anger probably is repressing awfully hard and is not to be trusted. I sincerely believe that most people have a sense of humor and do find those things funny; if they don't laugh, then they are repressing and probably for the wrong reasons. Many of those who don't laugh feel they are on God's side and to offend God is to offend them. Heaven save me from people totally certain they have a pipeline to God.

Let me here inject an aside that I have on extremely rare occasions found a few "good guys" who do not find dirty jokes funny and who do not even laugh politely at them. One of my oldest and best friends fails to see the humor in them because he says—and rightly—that jokes of all types usually involve pain for someone, and that pain is not funny. So there are a few, a very few people whom you can trust who do not laugh at jokes. However, it should be noted that they do not turn up their noses at them on moral grounds.

Another category of people, even worse than the first in my book, is those who snicker at dirty jokes. These are the ones who find such humor deliciously dirty. I knew a fellow a few years ago—in fact, he was my boss at the time—who always snickered and twittered when something off-color was mentioned. He was like a little child doing something his mother had told him not to do and was immensely proud of himself. People like this are the first to put the knife in your back—which is exactly what he did to me at the first opportunity.

No, give me a man who enjoys an outright belly laugh at a dirty joke. These are the ones you can trust as good, solid old boys. Of course, there is one other category: the ones who don't get the point of a dirty joke. These you should not trust either, for they generally are either very sheltered or else awfully dumb.

ACCOUNTABILITY

For years the public has been wanting—and recently demanding—that higher education become more accountable for the dollars it spends and for what it is doing to the students who use its services. Now, suddenly, academicians have discovered the word "accountability" and are turning it into yet another of their catch-phrases. The word has supplanted "excellence," which reigned for several years, and "relevance," which was the next most recent jargon word. Just as everyone was searching for relevance until two years ago, now everyone is hustling to be accountable. The irony here, of course, is that we now are about as likely to get accountability from scholars as we were to get excellence and relevance.

Scholars have never wanted to be accountable, but they have had the concept forced upon them by their constituents. It came from legislators in the many states where bills have been introduced to force a twelve-hour load on all faculty. This was and is being done because of the mistaken belief that making academicians spend more hours in the classroom will make them work harder. Here in my own state, when such a bill was introduced, I read it closely and with great interest. And I was delighted with it, for the bill provided that for each graduate student a professor was directing he got a specified reduction in teaching load. Because of the number of graduate students working under my direction, I would have been teaching no classes at all if the bill had become the law.

But increasing the work load of the professor without graduate students from six hours a week to twelve hours a week will not make him more accountable for the salary he receives. In fact, it probably will make him less so, for working him in four classes instead of two means only that he has to read his yellowed lecture notes to a greater number of students than previously; thus he can do even greater harm by making yet more people hate the university.

What then does accountability mean if not the number of hours the professor works? It means many things *but to different people*. To the alumnus accountability at the alma mater means having a winning football team. That is first. Second means having a sound public image so he can brag about the place he did his degree. To the citizens of the state it means having the school open to everyone, especially to their own children, but done at a cost that does not cause taxes to rise. This kind of mentality has been written into the law in every state, for the universities and colleges get their support from the state based on numbers; the more students, the more money they get. However, the cost of education is not a fixed quantity; it does not and cannot cost the same to educate every student at every institution. Some schools have more expensive programs, such as engineering, architecture, or medicine. And big schools cost progressively more to operate than small ones.

To the Department of Education in Washington, accountability means hiring a specified percentage of women and people from minority races. It means this often in the face of underqualification on the part of such aspiring professors. The Department of Education seems these days to be filled with idealistic do-gooders determined to use federal dollars as a club with which to beat the academic world into a new posture. However, they fail to realize that institutions such as my own, which anxiously want to hire more members of minority races, cannot compete financially with richer schools for the few qualified blacks, Chicanos, and Indians. I sometimes think that the racism of the past—and it did exist—is as nothing to the present reverse racism. Now an extremely well-qualified white man doesn't have a chance.

Accountability, to many professors, means keeping a low teaching load so that they can get grant money; it means pulling in students so they can create more jobs; it means fighting the administration. In short, they see themselves as accountable to their fellow academicians for upholding the cushy position to which most of them feel entitled.

Finally, to the students accountability means two things simultaneously—and these are in conflict with one another. It means that the professors should be forced to pass all of them willy-nilly, work or no work, learning or no learning; yet it also means that they all want to get high-paying jobs the minute they walk across the stage at commencement. These two goals are incompatible, for to get good jobs these students must learn something—which only a few will do unless forced into it.

True accountability—which is what both the public and academicians say they want—if it is not teaching load or winning athletic teams or easy grades, is really *effective* teaching. Making the student *learn* something, preferably something useful in getting a job or at least in humanizing him. But there will never be true accountability on college campuses because incompetence is protected by that wonderful thing known as tenure. Wretched professors cannot be fired (see the chapter on firing). If we are ever to arrive at a point of true accountability, we must devise some yardstick that measures effective teaching. We have to attract good instructors to the profession, reward them, run off the incompetents, and give raises only on the basis of merit. Surely a profession with as many know-it-alls as college teaching is capable of devising some means of measuring effective teaching.

On the other hand I am no advocate of the outright abolition of tenure. The absence of that protection can lead to terrible abuses at both public and private colleges and universities. In the state schools without such protection, politicians can decide at their own whim who can teach and what will be taught—and the reverse. I remember an example of this that occurred in the Midwest; in one state there, the governor elected in 1930 for a four-year term personally took a hand in firing many professors from college campuses, for that state at the time had no constitutional board of regents or tenure laws to hinder the man. Once he fired the people he called incompetent, he replaced them with men whose only qualifications were political connection and friendship. The result, of course, was not conducive to education.

And I recall a story about a private, fundamental, denominational university in another state where a member of the history department got to figuring out the size of Noah's Ark from the dimensions given in the Bible; after computing all this, he announced that the Ark obviously was too small to have held two of every specie of animal, bird, and insect. For his labors he was fired, a simultaneous warning to the rest of the faculty to avoid religious deviation and working in mathematics without a degree in that subject.

Therefore the tenure system is good, but it should be one based on real merit, not awarded for meeting classes for three, four, or six years.

And there is the reverse side of the coin. Just as some profs should be run off, so also should some students. The public must be made aware that not everyone can or should go to college. Everyone should have the opportunity to attend, but those students who fail to take advantage of the privilege should be encouraged, even forced to leave. Education is a privilege, not a right.

I think part of the reason for the current public drive to obtain accountability is that professors have abused their privileges. They have been guilty of multiple sins of omission and commission. And another part of the trouble is that college graduates are having difficulty finding employment here in the 1970s. Parents who have paid the horrendous costs of financing four years at some institution of higher learning for their children are outraged when Little Johnny or Sweet Mary cannot get a job that makes him or her an instant millionaire—or even earn a decent living. A generation and more ago a college degree did enable its holder to move up in society rapidly. Today, however, more and more people have college degrees (I had one of these bright lads a few days ago ask me if I realized how many holes there would be on our administration building lawn if someone would just come along and take the dirt out of them); and because there are so many people with a B.A. or B.S.—and because the curriculum has been so watered down that a college degree has become somewhat cheap—employers no longer are lining up to hire these people. A movement started several years ago in the public schools to pass everyone, social promotion it was called, has now reached into many colleges and universities, and the result has been the graduation of too many who cannot read and write, who cannot do simple sums in arithmetic, and who cannot think logically.

These faults are not exclusive to small colleges or big colleges. They are true across the board. A student can get just as good an education at Podunk State College as he can at Yale or Harvard or some Ivy League institution. Possibly even a better education at the small school, for there he prob-

99

ably will not be filled with delusions of superiority. He will have to work to get the education at Podunk State, perhaps ever harder than at Yale because the level of competition is lower, but gaining an education anywhere is work.

Accountability is no magic word. The public demanding it will not accomplish it, nor will scholars echoing the demand by making it a catch phrase make it happen immediately. We will achieve it only by devising an accurate means of measuring performance in the classroom, in research, in extension, and in other facets of education. Once these are devised, they should be applied and applied hard. Fire the incompetent, the man who has died but who will not lay down until age sixty-five. Give raises only to those who merit them. The old economic incentive is not a bad one. People will work harder for more money, even scholars mouthing phrases about the evils of materialism. Pay the good ones extra and the poor ones little, and the gap will narrow between bad and good in a way definitely positive. And if the school employing the professor is too poor to pay off in money, pay in prestige. It is amazing how hard people will work for an honorific title or some kind of recognition at commencement.

It has been said that in a democracy people get the kind of government they deserve. If this same adage holds true for education, it is a sad commentary about the United States today. I think accountability is a good idea. Let's apply it to colleges and universities—and to legislators and plumbers and carpenters and auto manufacturers and....

IV
A Look at Four Areas

THE ARTS

In America—and, I suspect, in most of the world—much of what passes for "culture" in the arts is that which is a commercial flop. It fails for a very good reason: too few people like it. This at once is the curse of the arts and the blessing. If people in large numbers did actually like "good art" and "good music" and "good drama," then the beautiful few who support chamber music groups, opera companies, art shows, and experimental theater would no longer shell out their money. These culture maniacs dote on words like avant-garde, improvisational, experimental, and controversial. They pride themselves on being a cultural minority, these self-styled intellectuals. They are masochists who delight, even need, to profess to like what saner folks know to be phony—and often a put-on.

Recently I was talking with one of the beautiful people. She was from Boston. We were discussing her home town, and I told her I thought it dirty, polluted, and crowded and that its inhabitants were incredibly pushy. To this she replied that all this was true but that Boston offered a great symphony and many cultural opportunities, all of which she helped support. I then asked her how often she attended these festivities. "Rarely," she finally admitted. "But I have to know they are available." The truth is she probably hates the symphony and the opera and much of the theater. The art on the walls of her office was of the modernistic type, swirls of color and blobs of paint. Of course, this was to prove that she was appreciative of the finer things.

"Artists" cash in on these culture maniacs by selling them what really is nothing more than junk. Basically most modern artists working in the medium of paint and canvas have no real artistic talent, or if they do it is very much undeveloped. They have never learned to draw. They do not know perspective or harmony or composition or balance. They cannot draw a realistic figure of a man or a horse or a flower or anything else. So they make a virtue of their lack of talent or training. They swirp and swipe blotches of color or lines—or paint a single black dot on a white canvas and give it some wild title like "Away to Infinity."

When the mass of people laugh at such efforts, these artists swear that only the culturally educated, only someone with taste, is capable of understanding what they are doing. The truth is that the great unwashed herd does understand what these "artists" are doing—which is running a con game. Such must be the case when chimpanzees win art contests.

And the culture maniacs love it. They look at a picture of assorted lines and jumbled colors and say the artist emotes strong feeling or that the picture has symbiotic harmony or some such meaningless remark. They say it evokes a mood or that it communicates with something basic—whatever that means. And they pay inflated prices for the junk. They buy it to hang in their homes as a badge of culture (and drive their children and pets to psychiatrists) or else purchase it to donate it to some museum or another that has sprung up to pander to the beautiful people with more money than sense.

Yet the true purpose of real art is to communicate. No more and no less. And the more people to whom a painting speaks—not the fewer—the greater is the art. I recall once viewing some blotchy monstrosity and voicing just such thoughts to an acquaintance who considered himself arty. He was shocked at my heresy. "What kind of art do you prefer?" he asked. I told him Charles Russell or some other realistic painter of Western scenes. "The trouble with you is that you want to be spoonfed," he responded with heat and anger.

The same situation is true in the field of sculpture where too many artists work with coathangers and wirecutters to produce modules or else arc weld scraps of metal together into some formless blob and call it "Prometheus With a Fire Extinguisher" or some such. Playwrights with no talent turn out heavy and dreary plays staged once and then sent quietly to a deserved early retirement. Composers whose only qualifications seem to be long hair and an aversion to soap compose "good music" that no one can stand to hear.

And the federal government subsidizes that kind of thing. Several small colleges, thanks to federal or private grants, have a "composer in residence" or "poet in residence." I remember when I was in graduate school that the city public schools had a composer in residence, thanks to a Ford Foundation grant. And he delivered a composition that year, a symphony for French horn. I attended the rendition of the piece—and cannot forget the incident. Either the French horn player was hit in the lip by the door as he came to the evening's performance or else the entire composition was written off-key. It was horrible.

I firmly believe that the reason so few artists today have any real talent is because those with that rare commodity are working in industry. There is more true art in a refrigerator than most of what is on canvas, in an automobile than in sculpture, in a television commercial jingle than in our "good music." The real artists of our age are in industrial design, advertising layout, and commercial music—for that is where the money is.

Contrary to what most people think about artists, the real ones go for the money and the prestige, not for the garret and starving and obscurity. They go to Detroit and design new Chevrolets and Fords rather than trying to making a living painting for shows; they go the New York to work for an advertising agency doing layouts rather than sit around in small towns giving lessons to unwilling children and trying to sell an abstract to decorate someone's living room; they design washing machines and new electric steam irons rather than sit on the square in the French Quarter in New Orleans trying to sell something to tourists; they compose a tune designed to sell a soft drink or a line of men's underwear rather than composing symphonies.

The great tragedy of all this focuses on college campuses where a real artistic revolution might be wrought. For it is to the college campus that the third-rate artists too often move. The first-class ones are in commercial art; the second-rate ones are slopping pictures together for the culture maniacs; that leaves the third-rate ones to teach that which they cannot do for money.

Yet at the same time there are many young people who come to college wanting to study art and who really want to learn to draw. They want to gain skills in basic composition and color harmony and balance and perspective. They want to learn to work with oils and water colors and charcoal, not just with acrylics (which is the current rage with the no-talent crowd). However, when these students arrive on campus, they are not taught; they are told instead to paint "what they feel." Just express yourself, say instructors who have never learned the basics of their craft.

Similarly our college drama departments all too often stage "serious" plays instead of theater that would attract a new generation of theater-goers. Our music departments train "serious" musicians, not those who might give real pleasure to the majority of our citizens. If colleges and universities would seek out talented people and hire them as professors, they in turn might educate a new generation of artists who see their craft as one of communication rather than the opposite. And the public does want and need art in all its many forms—and is too smart to believe that a swirl of acrylic constitutes great and enduring art (I base this opinion on the widespread sale of prints of the great art of a century ago; go into most people's homes and look at what is framed on the wall); they know that a song performed by a 101-piece symphony is not necessarily great and that a new play is not worth nine dollars a seat just because everyone in it curses and has long hair.

The common answer from "modern artists" is that a camera can take a picture more accurate than they can paint it and thus there is no longer any need for realistic art, and that their new dramas must reflect "real life." Do not believe it. Such is the false claim of people with no talent. For example, in painting realistically the true artist improves on reality or condenses it to drive home a point that otherwise might be missed—or simply make the scene more enjoyable. All art does not have to have a message; some of it can be for pure enjoyment.

Only when a generation of true artists is trained by our colleges and universities will we get away from pictures of blobs with eyeballs in their navels or in the middle of their noses, and from statues mistakenly hauled away to the junk yard before they can be exhibited because the junkman was a better art critic than those exhibiting the work.

Yet to accomplish this will require courage on the part of college administrators. These overworked individuals generally do not profess to be art or drama or music critics and therefore have to rely on their professors—who for the most part are from the no-talent crowd. And this group of professors fights viciously to keep out anyone with talent or ability or training. I know firsthand of one artist of exceptional talent who suffered for his rising popularity. He painted Western pictures of enduring appeal, and he was selling well enough to gain a growing reputation. His colleagues refused to vote him tenure and he was forced to leave the institution for his sins—which were: he had talent, he was a genuine artist, the students liked him, and the public was giving him increased recognition. For these things he was forced from

106

the professorial world.

And in this move the professors were supported by the culture snobs of the state. To cries that the public liked that man's work, the intellectuals responded, "The public has no taste." I note that the public had enough taste to be paying the salaries of those professors—and that gives the public the right to judge who it wants teaching at the institution. I believe the administrators at that college should have fired the rest of the faculty, kept the good one, hired more like him, and started a school devoted to representational art. If they had done that, they would be overrun with students, so many that soon other colleges would be following their "innovational" approach. Who knows? The result might have been a return to real art and a bringing of art to the masses—which is what the intellectuals claim to want to do!

THE HUMANITIES

Four professors and four students, all from a department mistakenly labeled "Humanities" were sitting together as a formal committee. Their task was to find ways to make students more aware of "good" music and art and drama. Suggestions came thick and fast. Make each student sit through certain drama productions; have them go into the audio visual laboratory and listen to "good" music; require them to attend the showing of selected arty films.

Finally an invited guest at this committee meeting, a man with more sense than discretion, asked, "How are you going to take some country boy raised on the Grand Old Opry and make him like string quartet music from the 17th century? By telling him it is 'good' music?"

The Humanists raised their eyebrows in horror. "But we've got to educate them to appreciate the good things of life! We have to instil a sense of esthetics in them!"

The visitor, a professor from another department, tried his best to educate the Humanists. "Some of those old country boys have very high intelligence quotients. They're smart. And they think they have taste. Yet you are going to sit them down in class, tell them what they like is bad and that what you like is good. And then you're going to force them to listen to what you think they should listen to, sit through plays you think are good, see films you think are artistic. The students will think you're the one without taste. Oh, you can force him into these assignments and you can make him do these things. But the end result will be that he will hate you, hate the university, and hate ever more the type of music and art and drama and films you want him to like."

Of course, speaking such truth to Humanists does not make anyone popular with them. Yet the truth is, they take a very heavy-handed approach with their students, and generally they do end up making the students hate "good" humanistic works. I rarely have met one of these birds who has sufficient taste to like country and western music or the Nashville sound; in fact, none of them wants to admit that he likes popular music. No, on his stereo set at his home you find Mozart concertos, fugues by Bach, or variations by Vivaldi. The only concession to the 20th century these people make is to play a little cool jazz every now and then.

These are the same people who try to make opening night for university drama productions. And they exclaim with delight about how wonderful a play is if it is some obscure modern drama about people with bad breath and world-savior complexes. Yet at one university where I was teaching, I decided I would like to see *Cyrano de Bergerac* performed, inasmuch as this is one of the truly conservative plays of modern times; it is conservative in that it speaks to something forever young in us all, an enduring quality that unites humanity of all eras and ages. The director of drama at this institution wrote me back to say that in her seventeen years at that university, mine was the first request by a member of the faculty to have a play staged. Yet at every one of her productions—and she is a noted drama professor—I saw these Humanists parading around, there to be seen rather than to see. The play itself was unimportant to them. All they wished to do was to prove they had taste.

Nor do these guardians of public taste ever admit to watching television. I recall one such individual who, believe it or not, bought a portable television set and kept it on a stand with rollers; this he kept in his closet, rolling it out to watch everything scheduled, but if the doorbell rang he could wheel it swiftly inside the closet, shut the door, and tell one and all he "never watched television."

As an English minor through college at the bachelor's, master's, and doctoral level, I am aware of the continuing argument about what makes great literature "great." I recall the argument that public taste is set by the "passionate few"—those self-appointed guardians of Western culture who see themselves as the only ones with taste and culture; they are the professors and critics and writers who keep telling the public over and over again what is "good." These are the people who award enduring greatness to some author or composer. Why do students in high school keep having to read Shakespeare or Shelley? Certainly not because they like it or appreciate it or think it is good. Rather it is because the "passionate few" are in a position to select what is included in their books.

Well, poets and playwrights are a doubtful breed whose relative merits I prefer to judge for myself. My quarrel with the Humanists is that they want to set themselves up as judges for the world. In short, they want to enforce their beliefs on me and you and not keep them to themselves. They are entitled to their opinions, but why should they be allowed to foist these off on unwitting and unwilling students?

And these are the very people who fight to get onto the General Studies Committee where the rules are made about the courses that all university students *must* take. Every university, under one name or another, has such a committee, and it decides on the courses required for every student going through, be he in engineering, the sciences, business, or the liberal arts; he must have so much English, history, science, math, etc. These Humanists actually want to be on these committees. There they speak about the freedom of choice and how each member of this committee should avoid working only for his own discipline—and then they fight like tigers to get Humanities courses listed under every conceivable category. They well know that if they do not, the students will not by choice elect to take their courses.

Ah, God, what a frustration it must be for these people. They alone have "taste" and "culture." They alone know what is "good" for the world. But the world does not listen. Well, then, it must be bludgeoned into listening. Force them to take our courses. Work our way into the textbook field and slip our message in where they must go through it. James Bond, move over, the Humanists are here, theirs a mission more important than mere patriotism; theirs a divine mandate to be dictator of public taste. "Give us the reins, and by God, we'll drive the wagon!"

Such people frighten me just a little.

Besides that, they are cheap. The members of one Humanities department of which I know wanted to read my previous book on the world of professors (*This Beats Working for a Living*), but they did not want to pay $5.95 apiece. So each chipped in 30 or 40 cents and they bought a departmental copy; this was passed from faculty member to faculty member on a circulating library basis until all had read it—and hated me. Cheap! I wonder which one of them ended up with the copy. Probably some philosopher.

Now there's a special category by itself—the philosophy instructors at universities. I know that history professors refer to themselves as historians and people in physics as physicists, but I have yet to meet someone teaching philosophy who by any stretch of the imagination should call himself a philosopher. The dictionary definition of a philosopher is someone who applies the rules of philosophy to his life or one with a strong knowledge of philosophy. It is not, as you might believe, someone who *thinks* or has weighty thoughts; there they certainly would fail. Yet they also fail on the first point; they do not apply what they teach to their own lives—I rarely have met anyone as illogical as a professor of philosophy. Too many of them are renegade ministers unable to secure employment in any other line of endeavor.

Out of curiosity I started talking to students who have suffered through a philosophy course to get reactions. "Boring," I was told. Wretched, dull, idiotic—such were the adjectives. Others laughed at instructors whose lectures were built around a discourse on whether or not an axe was an axe if it had never been used to chop wood, or if a tree falling in the forest made any noise if no one was around to hear it. But my favorite is the philosophy instructor who told of some nutty philosopher who once dreamed he was a butterfly, then spent the rest of his life wondering if he was a man who had dreamed he was a butterfly—or a butterfly who was dreaming he was a man.

One student told me of a philosophy instructor who walked back and forth in front of the class, his hand under his chin in the classical pose of Rodin's statue of "The Thinker." I guess this fellow believed he would have great thoughts strike him if he assumed the pose of a philosopher (see the chapter on role playing).

I guess what I am trying to say here is that I have rarely met someone in the Humanities department whom I would hire to think, or whom I would want instructing my children in the art. They teach about ideas, but have none; they discuss great music but have never made any; they lecture about literature but seem only semiliterate; they call themselves teachers but cannot teach. Diogenes certainly would not find his honest man amidst their ranks much as they prattle about him and his quest. They are mere semanticists playing with words.

Yet they see themselves as sophisticated and the rest of the world as clods. They should look in the dictionary at the definition of the word sophisticated, for it comes from the same root word as sophistry—which has to do with trickery and deception. Sadly, these people have most deceived themselves.

ATHLETICS

Young boys are an aggressive—some might even say an obnoxious—lot. Contrary to what the fem-lib types might like to believe, boys apparently are born with more aggressive tendencies than girls; this is not something learned but rather innate. Society has found a way to channel this aggressiveness through organized sports, although it might be debated whether athletics channels a natural tendency or if it encourages something which otherwise might die.

However, as society is now structured, boys are encouraged by their fellows as well as their fathers to join in organized sports. Moreover, they are taught from the days of little league baseball and peewee football that the only true glory is in winning. One well-known football coach is supposed to have said that winning may not be everything but it beats hell out of anything connected with coming in second. Such also is society's attitude—and I am not against it; life is competitive, and young boys might as well learn it early.

No young fellow escapes the pressure to join in sports. Fat, unathletic boys are made to feel second-class citizens, failures in life before they reach the ripe old age of sixteen, while those lads too young to participate as yet can prepare themselves by collecting baseball or football cards acquired from packages of bubble gum; they can begin memorizing all the statistics about Hank Aaron and Mickey Mantle or Johnny Unitis and Bart Starr. In the summer they can join in recreation league competition, and in the fall and spring they can represent their elementary or junior high school in interscholastic games. Boys with only second-rate ability virtually kill themselves trying to excell, while those with natural-born athletic ability become kings in their own right.

Yet, as most boys enter college, or at least shortly thereafter, they begin to realize their limitations. Few of them have the ability to become professional athletes; except for these favored few, life gives its economic rewards to those of mental rather than physical ability. Thus the great majority of young adult males in college and afterward concentrate primarily at winning in the business or professional world.

However, even the majority of men, those realizing their limitations, still dream of athletic glory. They still strain themselves playing paddle ball or handball or golf or tennis. They swim twenty laps a day or run several miles. Doctors encourage this type of activity by stating that physical activity will increase the lifespan. I am reminded here of Thomas Jefferson and James Madison, two Virginia contemporaries. Jefferson was a great believer in physical fitness and exercized two hours every day, while Madison, a sickly, weak person, avoided such activity. Jefferson lived to be eighty-three—while Madison made it to eighty-seven.

Moreover, most men find it difficult to admit that advancing age has diminished their athletic ability. Old duffers of forty and more still join in the annual picnic baseball game or touch football game. Every fall at this university campus I see professors with arms or legs in casts acquired from some athletic endeavor. One friend of mine joined the department's softball team (made up of graduate students and young professors); I kidded him that at thirty-four he was too old for such antics, but he assured me he was physically capable. "Why, I'm just in my prime," he stated. But a couple of weeks later he was playing in a game and broke three bones in his right foot trying to round third and get home. I derived some cruel satisfaction in saying, "I told you so." He finally admitted that he was getting on toward middle age and that softball was beyond him. "Hereafter," he said dolefully, "I'm going to confine myself to nothing more strenuous than golf."

Even those men smart enough to realize that a middle-aged man cannot play active sports unless he has done so continuously from an early age still often are enthralled with sports in a vicarious way. They watch all the ball games on television—baseball, football, basketball, hockey, wrestling; they watch collegiate and professional sports alike, and they go to all the games within commuting distance. I even have known a graduate student or two who flunked out of college because he spent too much time watching our local football gladiators practicing every day.

Yes, most males are enthralled with competitive sports although they do not make their living at them. Oh, they are willing to spend endless time talking sports—listen to their conversation at cocktail parties and at coffee break; the fellow who can't Monday-Morning-Quarterback a team is considered something less than a real man. And the older many men get, the more enthused they get about sports; I know some old men of seventy and more who almost have a heart attack if their alma mater loses the Saturday big game.

The result of all of this is an extraordinary amount of pressure on colleges and universities to produce winning teams in every sport. In the good old days of ten or fifteen years ago, football was the only sport that really mattered. The basketball coach and the baseball coach performed their tasks with few people on the campus really noticing them; win or lose, it was all the same. Now, however, every coach, from wrestling to tennis to golf to swimming, has to have a winner.

And while the alumni are bringing pressure from one direction for the old school to produce a winning team with which they can identify, the athletes themselves are bringing pressure on the coaches. Television has made professional athletics in several categories—baseball, football, basketball, even golf—highly profitable, and almost every kid who signs up to play in any sport at a college nowadays has visions of a multimillion dollar contract to be signed when he completes his four years of eligibility (notice I did not say "graduation," for many of the college super athletes do not graduate—even have no intention of graduating). Therefore they refuse to go to a school not producing winning teams capable of attracting the attention of the professional scouts.

And there also is pressure on college coaches to win, win, win because to do so can mean a great deal of money for the school. Legislators appropriating money have a way of being more generous with those universities that have winning athletic teams than those with losing teams. Moreover, the old grads seem more generous in their donations to the alma mater when it has a winning team than when it has a losing one. Even the most absent-minded member of the philosophy department at most schools has figured out that it is more to his benefit if the local warriors win on the gridiron than if they lose. Thus the faculty likewise is pressuring the coach to

114

win, win, win.

The end result of all these pressures is that coaching today has got to be one of the hardest jobs around. Coaches are running what amounts to minor league professional sports, but not in the business world where people realize the direct connection between investing money and getting a winning team. Often coaches are expected to produce a team picked in the top twenty in the nation but with no financial backing. They are expected to recruit all the blue-chip players from high school ranks, but with little or no budget for recruiting.

And these coaches live in a cut-throat world where the fans have an extremely short memory. I recall one coach who for three years produced winning teams that were ranked nationally, and then he had an off year; immediately the alumni were demanding his resignation, while the local students were burning him in effigy.

And the coach lives in a world where there are very few top jobs. In a state such as Texas, for example, there are some 4,500 high school coaches, but only six or eight really good coaching jobs. The competition for one of these positions, when one comes open, is extremely keen, especially when you consider that the committee seeking a replacement also looks out-of-state as well as in-state. The coach lives in a dog-eat-dog world in which statistically only half the teams can have a winning season in any given year, and only one team in any conference can be the conference champion. Moreover, to gain any real fame the coach has to win his conference title several years in a row.

For the few coaches who do make it to the top in the university world—that is, they become head coach at a name school in a name conference—the pace is extremely hectic. And the coach finds that he no longer really is coaching. He has an assistant to coach the backfield, another for the line, and a third for the defense; he has yet more assistants to coach the freshmen and to do his recruiting. The head coach has become a super salesman for his program and for his institution, the star attraction at any gathering of the alumni and the darling of Rotary clubs in all the nearby cities. He may even have his own television show; in fact, that is a prime fringe benefit for university coaches, for it is one way to supplement their income. At one institution at which I taught we lost our head coach to another school where the local television show paid better than did ours (and some of these pay incredibly well; I heard of one coach who receives $48,000 for his television series each fall).

Yes, the coach's world is one of great pressure, great frustration, and rapid changes. Today's hero is tomorrow's goat. Lose just a few of the big games, and the students, the alumni, even the local businessmen go after his scalp with a viciousness that would please Ivan the Terrible. And so the pressure is continual. There never is any resting on laurels. He has to win this year, recruit the best possible material, hire good assistants to train them, get some of his former students into the professional ranks, and win again next year. Otherwise he heads for the unemployment line.

All this would not be so bad except that the coach has to do this on a college campus where all the intellectuals sneer at "athletes and athletics." Coaches' wives are not always welcomed into the faculty wives' club with any warmth, while the coaches themselves are treated as country cousins at faculty gatherings.

My best advice to potential coaches—that is, to college athletes—is to take a few courses in college on the selling of insurance. Many coaches every year grow tired of the pressures and the rat race and get out, a large number to sell insurance. However, a really good coach can do a university a great amount of financial good, just as he has a rare opportunity to help young men.

THE COMMUNICATIONS GAP

I recently was talking with some of my graduate students, young people who aspire to write, and I pointed out to one of them that in the paper he had handed in to me he had a split infinitive (among other mistakes). "What is a split infinitive?" he asked. I was struck speechless, for that fellow was an English minor.

Curious now, I asked him to explain the eight parts of speech to me. "But I never learned those," he told me.

"What did they teach you in freshmen English," I asked, for that is the course where the student is supposed to learn grammar and composition.

"Oh, that was a good course," he told me. "The first day of class the instructor had us stand up and walk around in the room until we found someone whose vibrations felt good. Naturally we all found someone of the opposite sex. Then he had one person out of each of these pairs blindfolded, and the other one led him across campus blindfolded." I asked the purpose of this exercise. "It was to show us that we could trust someone," he told me.

I thought about this for some time, finally wondering if all the pairs of students made it back to the class—and what the heck this had to do with freshman grammar and composition. It sounded more like some kind of sensitivity session than anything to do with verbs and nouns and commas.

But apparently this is the new wave among English teachers, and it explains why in recent years there has been a great deal of talk about the various gaps that afflict us. You know, the "generation gap" and the "credibility gap." Actually, all of these things really are "communications gaps." Our high schools, along with too many of our colleges and universities, are turning out generations of semiliterates and downright illiterates. Too many students walk across the commencement stage unable to write clearly and explicitly what they mean or think, nor can they read the printed page and tell you what the author was trying to communicate. This is not just in the sciences and engineering, but across the board.

And the failure here is not altogether that of the student, but usually is the fault of the English teacher. At both the public school and college level those responsible for teaching grammar do not drill and work their students and require them to learn something in order to pass. I once had the questionable pleasure of teaching seventh-grade English, and most of what I taught—the eight parts of speech and how to use them, punctuation, grammar, composition, etc.—is also taught at the eighth, ninth, tenth, eleventh, and twelfth grades in the public schools, as well as in freshman grammar and composition courses in college. At least, this is what should be taught; in theory students are exposed to this material a total of seven times by my count.

Instead, professors of English, most of them frustrated writers of fiction, concentrate on the *meaning* of the poetry, stories, essays, plays, and novels that the students are assigned to read. "What was the author really saying?" these professors ask their students. And then the students, who are not dummies, think up the wildest possible things, and the discussion lasts until the bell rings. "In Mark Twain's *Huckleberry Finn,*" say the professors, "the Mississippi River represents God, and Huck's attachment to Jim is symbolic of homosexuality." I recall Mark Twain's own comment about this subject: "The critic's symbol should be the tumble-bug: he deposits his egg in somebody else's dung, otherwise he could not hatch it." (The same thing might well be said of book reviewers, but that is another story.)

The sad part of this is that the English professor, when he is quoting all these great theories about what Shakespeare really meant when he wrote *The Merchant of Venice* or *Julius Caesar,* is just quoting ideas about the work which he read in some academic journal devoted to literature. When he expounds so learnedly on Faulkner's "two levels of meaning going in opposite directions," he is telling you what some professor wrote in *Publications of the Modern Language Association.* Most of these people have not had an original idea in their lives, would not even recognize one if it kicked them hard, and will not tolerate original thinking on the part of their students.

I have a friend (one of the two to whom this book is dedicated) who years ago was an English major and who was

118

taking a course on Shakespeare. In class he was assigned to do a paper on *Henry IV: Part One*. He turned in his thoughts on the subject, but the professor had, from his reading of learned journals, a different view of the play. Therefore he assigned a low grade to the student and held him up to ridicule in class. My friend then did two things: he changed his major, and he submitted his paper on *Henry IV* to a scholarly journal of literature. It was accepted and published—and doubtless thereafter the professor who had taught the course began teaching my friend's interpretation of *Henry IV* as the correct one.

Nor do English professors as a group have a great sense of humor. I once heard what I considered to be a pretty good joke and passed it along to a fellow who taught Shakespeare courses. The joke involved a young man who always wanted to be an actor, but college drama classes and acting schools failed to win him a chance to tread the boards. Then his father died and left him millions, whereupon he hired some actors, rented a theater, and readied a presentation of *Hamlet* with himself in the lead. He even had a public relations firm ballyhoo the production— and give away loads of free tickets—so that on opening night the theater was filled. It quickly became apparent, when the curtain raised, why this fellow had never been on the stage, and the actors he had been able to hire were equally fifth-rate. The audience began to mutter, then boo, and finally to throw rotten vegetables, but the man in question sailed right on through the role of Hamlet. At last he reached the soliloquy, at which point some poor fellow in the audience, who could not stand the butchering of Shakespeare's work, jumped up, ripped his chair cushion loose, and threw it, hitting "Hamlet" right in the face. That stopped the play as "Hamlet" ran his hand across his forehead to see if there was any blood; then walked up to the footlights and addressed the audience: "Dear and gentle folks, be patient. Be kind. You have to remember, I didn't write this crap."

The English professor to whom I told this story looked at me a long moment. "That's sick!" he muttered and walked away. I had spoken heresy.

Young, aspiring writers, even would-be poets, sign up for courses with men like that, listen to interpretations and even learn to make them—but they never learn grammar, to say nothing of creativity. At last they receive a degree and go out into the world to teach "interpretation" to high school students, not grammar, or else they stay in college to get a master's degree or a doctorate and teach interpretation at that level. But they never teach grammar and composition because none of them know any.

A group of fellow historians and I were talking about this situation, and somehow the subject came up of what one would call a group of English professors. A herd, a gang, a flock, a pack? At last, we discerned, one properly should refer to a "Pride of Historians" and a "Gaggle of English professors."

If this sounds hard on the professors who are supposed to teach grammar, I mean for it to. I blame them for students' failure to learn grammar, because students will work as hard as they have to; if these teachers required students to learn grammar, then they would. Yet this is not a case of "those who can, do; those who can't, teach." Rather it is a case of those not knowing grammar being assigned to teach the subject and then talking about literary interpretation. The result is widespread illiteracy.

V

A Fable
(With Deep Meaning)

OLD WILLIE'S REVENGE

The searing heat of a summer Saturday afternoon pressed down mercilessly on the little West Texas farm and ranch community. The sidewalks were blinding reflectors of the dazzling sunlight, and the weekend shoppers took as long as possible to make their purchases in the air-conditioned stores. There was little hurrying, pushing, or wasted motion.

A quiet backwater to the economic activity was the east side of the county courthouse where the men gathered to take advantage of the shade. There they discussed crops, weather, and local news. The younger men stood around in small groups by themselves, or they hovered silently on the edges of the gatherings of the senior members of the community. The two cement benches under the shade trees on the lawn drew such circles of old-timers, but the prize position was the steps leading into the architectural monstrosity called the courthouse. This little area belonged to the very oldest men and the best raconteurs. It was the very heart of the "split-and-whittle" gang.

As yet this particular Saturday afternoon, it was still early, and the talk had not centered on any one subject exclusively. One old-timer was monopolizing the conversation on the steps.

"Well," he drawled, "this old Model T came snortin' and poppin' and knockin' along, and this boy Ray—he was kind of a smart aleck—he called out, 'What'cha gonna thrash with that thing?' The feller that was drivin' it said, 'I think I'll just thrash right here if the grain's not too green.' He stopped that Model T and got out, and they started to fight. That feller that was drivin' bit off a part of Ray's ear and just whipped the tar outta him. That's when Ray lost that chunk outta his ear."

A nod of heads among the group's older members showed both that they agreed with the speaker and that they had either witnessed the episode or had heard about it several times before.

Conversation temporarily halted at that point as the oldest active man in the community slowly made his way up the sidewalk and seated himself in a space that had conspicuously been left vacant. He wore a khaki shirt and trousers, a battered hat of uncertain shape, and shoes that were a combination between dress wear and boots. His white hair vividly contrasted with the sun-reddened upper portion of his face. Below that was the stubble of several days' growth of whiskers, well stained with tobacco juice. Everyone in town referred to the old gentleman as Mr. Sego. His first name had long since been forgotten, and no one would have dared use it even if he had known it. Mr. Sego was the undisputed patriarch of the loungers who gathered on the courthouse steps.

By common consent those gathered on the steps waited quietly for Mr. Sego to indicate the topic for conversation this Saturday.

"Well, Old Willie's gone," he said at last, his words a pronouncement which made Little Willie Arnold's death official. By unspoken agreement Willie, known as Little Willie during his lifetime, became Old Willie now that he was dead.

"I guess he's down there tellin' the Devil how to save on his fuel bill," commented one old man whose thin frame and shaking voice clearly indicated that he would follow Old Willie within a short time. "There wasn't nobody in this county as tight as Old Willie," the speaker finished.

No one smiled at the remark. Instead there was a general nodding of heads in agreement. Another member of the group spoke up. "Feels like we've all joined the Devil today. It must be a hundred and five." Before anyone could interrupt him to comment on the weather, the speaker hurried on. "Yep, I guess Old Willie was about the closest feller I ever knew." He spoke as if he were an authority on the subject of misers. "Did you know he fed his hogs cow chips? He did for a fact! He said it was kind of a tonic for 'em. I never ate no meat at his place—course, I was never offered none—so I don't know if it tasted any different than regular hog meat, but his hogs was always as fat as they could be. He'd just let 'em run loose in his cow pen."

On the periphery of the group an overalled young man of forty-five or so, a man who fancied himself the town wit, exclaimed, "Why Old Willie was so tight he'd a drilled an oil well in the cemetery if he'd a thought it'd a done some good."

Silence greeted that remark. The older men conspicuously made no comment for several moments and looked off in the distance to show their disapproval for the young upstart's interruption of their conversation. The culprit shuffled his feet in embarrassment, realizing that he had broken a taboo of the group. To speak to the gathering on the courthouse steps, one had to be old enough to rate a seat.

After an uncomfortably long silence, Mr. Sego cleared his throat, an indication that he was about to speak. As he talked, only his moving lips and animated eyes seemed alive in his tanned, leathery face. "You know," he started slowly, almost lovingly, "when Old Willie came to this county, he only brought about a dozen layin' hens with him. Them were the days when you could get a good layin' hen for a quarter. Well, Old Willie didn't want to buy no meat, so to get lots of fryers he'd set his hens twice." Observing smiles on the faces

124

of some of the younger men on the fringe of his audience, Mr. Sego added, "That may sound funny to some of you, but I seen him do it. When one of his hens'd start cluckin' around, he'd grab her up and put her on a bunch of eggs. If he had two hens to have their chicks about the same time, he'd just slip the chicks out from under the one that had hers last and give 'em to the other hen. Then he'd put some more eggs under the one he'd taken the chicks from and just keep her a settin'. You can set a hen to death if you keep her at it that way. On the second batch of eggs you'd have to watch the hen good, or she'd slip off there to get somethin' to eat or a drink and'ud let the eggs get cold. When Old Willie was a settin' a hen twice and seen her off the nest too long, he'd holler at her and chunk her until she scooted right back up on them eggs."

Mr. Sego paused, then added in a tone that indicated he would tolerate no arguing, "If you just keep after an old hen like that, you can set her to death." He swung his gaze around the listening group as if daring contradiction. There was none. Each man there sat quietly enjoying a comfortable silence for several moments. Each was busy remembering Old Willie.

"You know, the thing that always bothered me about Old Willie," said one of the usually quiet members of the group, "was how he kept from meltin' on hot days like this. He'd come down here dressed in that old blue work shirt with the top button buttoned and wearin' that vest of his on the hottest day in July. And when he'd sit where you could see the tops of his socks, why there was long underwear tucked in 'em right in the middle of the summer. I don't guess he ever took off them longhandles. And you know, he always looked cool as a cucumber even with all them clothes on."

Mr. Sego spoke again, his old eyes glowing. He was feeling good, and his thoughts were on the beloved past. "Old Willie was always close with his money. I remember one time he nearly bawled over a few dollars. He told me about it just after it happened. I guess this was back in '27 'cause that was the year I bought the Old Gammil place just outside of town—I wanted to get nearer to town to let my daughter go to high school. You remember my daughter Lettie. She's teachin' school down in Dallas now. Well, it was that year that Old Willie bought this little Jersey cow for eighty-five dollars. That was as pretty a Jersey cow as I ever seen. Maybe eighty-five dollars don't sound like much now, but that was a heap of money in them days. Anyhow, you know how a cow is when she wants to go dry. She'll lay out when it comes milkin' time. If cows ain't milked regular, they'll go dry. Well, usually cows'll come up when you whistle, but about once a month they try to miss so they'll go dry. One day Old Willie whistled through his teeth—I could whistle like that when I had my teeth—he whistled—you can hear a whistle like that for about half a mile—and this little Jersey cow didn't come up. She was down in one of his back pastures, so he sent his dog down after her. He had this bulldog that he kept to go down after cows and such. He didn't feed the dog nothin'—made it hunt for itself. When that dog went after a cow, he'd get around behind her and grab her by the tail right near the top and just hang on there. You've seen dogs do that. It always moves cows in a hurry. You know, cows get so when they see a dog a comin' they'll start movin' up to the barn. Well, this bulldog went down in the field where this Jersey cow was, but for some reason he didn't grab her by the tail. He got her by the upper hind leg instead, and somehow he bit right through the hamstring. That Jersey's leg gave a pop and sorta hung there limp. A knot came up on her that stuck out three or four inches. That cow got to where it could hardly move. Finally Old Willie sold her to a feller that ran a dairy up on the north side of town. This feller hayfed his cows so's they didn't have to do much walkin'. Old Willie'd give eighty-five dollars for that Jersey and hadn't had her more'n a month and a half, and he only got forty dollars for her. He cussed and carried on about that for a mighty long time, and it got to where ever' time he'd tell about it he'd nearly cry."

Another comfortable silence followed Mr. Sego's story.

Then Bud Thompson, although only seventy-three, offered a story. He was the second-longest resident in the county, having spent all but three of his years in the community, and therefore was well qualified to speak in this select group. As Bud talked, his ample stomach, which hung over a belt that struggled to hold up his khaki trousers, shook with pleasure.

"You know," he said, looking off into the distance as if he were actually viewing the scenes about which he spoke, "I remember the closest I ever came to seen' Old Willie cry was the time that boy of his found a stick of dynamite and a cap and decided to blow the porch off the little church where they went so's to scare ever'body." He paused and surveyed his audience. He must have decided that some explanation was needed. "Old Willie was so stingy he didn't marry till he was nigh fifty, and then it was to a schoolteacher, and you know what savin' ways old maid school teachers have. Vinnie Faye, that was her name. They only had one child, you know. I guess it's a good thing they didn't have no more, 'cause they sure made a mess of that one. That boy ain't worth a nickel. I don't reckon I ever saw a man come to dislike his own flesh and blood as much as Old Willie did that boy."

Bud paused a moment, but no one made an attempt to defend Old Willie's son. He continued, "Well, this boy Don Edward found a stick of dynamite and a cap and he decided to set it off under the porch on this church. Back in them days we didn't have no way to build a foundation 'cept to cut logs into about one-foot-long pieces and set them around and then build the house up on top them. You've seen old houses set up that way. That's the way this little church was built."

His explanation was hardly necessary. His audience knew about this early-day practice as well as the speaker, but there was no impatience with him for injecting it into this story. These old men loved their stories and preferred to have them lengthened.

"Well," Bud continued, "sure enough one Sunday mornin' when ever'one was in there and the preacher was a givin' em hell fire and brimstone and sayin' that one of these days this sinful old world was a goin' to come to an end, Don Edward set off that stick of dynamite under the porch, but instead of just blowin' off the porch like he figgered on doin', that whole building sorta gave a groan and rocked to one side, causin' them blocks to fall over. That old church hit the ground pretty hard. You can imagine what them folks inside musta thought. They musta thought the world was a comin' to an end. Either that or that a tornado'd hit. In either case they intended to git. They started pourin' outta windows and doors, scatterin' in ever' direction. That preacher, who'd just been tellin' how he was gonna be so happy when Judgment Day rolled around, he just jumped outta the back window and lit out runnin' like the Devil was a hangin' onto his coattails. I guess that boy had a good laugh at all the trouble he'd caused, but Old Willie, he was fit to be tied. Not 'cause he was ashamed or anything like that, but 'cause the deacons came 'round and told him he'd have to pay to get the church fixed up again. I guess that was about the only time I ever know'd him to whip that boy."

Mr. Sego, from the safety of his advanced years and senior status, contradicted Bud. "That wasn't the only time Old Willie whipped that boy. Once when Don Edward was about eighteen, he left the tractor parked out in the yard overnight. He always was about as lazy a boy as I ever knowed. The next mornin' Old Willie came out and his cows'd stripped ever' bit of insulation off the wires on that tractor. There ain't nothin' a cow loves better than to do that—or to lick the grease off a tractor. I remember one time I had a whole new can of grease that I'd just filled my grease gun one time out of. I left it out and forgot to put the lid back on it. Next mornin' when I came out, I could see my face in the bottom of it. The cows'd licked ever' bit of that grease up. Anyway, when Old Willie had to buy new wires for that tractor, he was so mad he gave that boy a good whippin'."

One old man who had said nothing all afternoon jumped into the silence that followed, offering still another story on Don Edward. "Back when that boy was about eight," he began, "Old Willie's relatives was a goin' to have a family get-together at his house. It was the first time that bunch'd all gathered at Willie's place. Well, sir, durin' the middle of the afternoon all the men was a standin' around in the yard tellin' stories and such, while the women was in the livin' room swappin' recipes and talkin' about their babies. The kids was all off by themselves playin', all 'cept that boy of Old Willie's. He wasn't with the others 'cause they didn't want him around. Directly Old Willie's wife, Vinnie Faye, says, 'I wonder what's happened to Don Edward. He's mighty quiet.' She got up to go see what that boy was up to. I guess it was Lester's wife—Lester was Willie's older brother that moved to Oklahoma—she went with Vinnie Faye, and she told it that they found that boy in the kitchen, and he'ud eaten a whole loaf of light bread. It seemed that he'd never seen any light bread before 'cause all they'd ever had durin' his whole lifetime was homemade biscuits and cornbread. Old Willie was so tight he'd never bought no store bread before, and that boy'd sat there and ate the whole loaf that they'd bought to feed at the family reunion. Yessir, that boy was always causin' Old Willie trouble."

The chuckles that followed this story did not mean that it was new. Probably most of the men there had heard it half a dozen times, but they always laughed when it was told.

By that time it was nearly six o'clock, and the crowd was thinning on the courthouse lawn. Younger men with families were leaving as their wives completed their shopping, but the regular crowd of loungers who had nothing to do until supper-time just made themselves more comfortable.

"I hear tell Old Willie had $75,000 stuck over there in the bank," commented one of those still there, a touch of envy in his voice. "Did he still have that much when he died?" someone asked.

"If he ever did have it, he did when he died," Bud Thompson declared. "That old man lived like a hog after his wife died. Why he was so tight he wouldn't buy nothin' but snuff. What tickles me is Willie's boy, Don Edward, waitin' around all these years to get his hands on that money and spend it. That boy ain't done enough work in his twenty-five years to hurt a flea. Why he'd a gone through that $75,000 like a dose of salts if Old

Willie hadn't a fooled him." Bud slapped his leg and laughed. "I guess ever'body was laughin' when they thought about Old Willie not spendin' a dime and savin' ever'thing he could beg, borrow, or steal. Why, after old tightwad stopped farmin' and moved into town, he mowed lawns so's not to have to spend any of the pension money he got from the government. Folks said that boy'd just spend all that money soon's Old Willie died, but ever'body, includin' Don Edward, was really surprised when the will was read yesterday."

"What'd it say?" asked one old man. "I was at the hospital all day yesterday and never did hear."

Bud slapped his leg again and chuckled. "I guess Old Willie had the last laugh, 'cause he fooled 'em all. He didn't leave a red cent more'n one dollar to that boy of his. He gave the rest of it to one of them church colleges down in Abilene. He said in his will that he was givin' it to them to make sure that Don Edward didn't get none of it, 'cause them college lawyers'd fight to keep it. And he said that by leavin' it to that college he know'd his boy wouldn't get no good out of it 'cause he was too lazy and sorry to go to college."

Silence followed as each of the old men enjoyed the way Old Willie had outsmarted his son. There was something richly satisfying to them about an older man outsmarting a younger one. After a few minutes Mr. Sego pulled himself erect and commented solemnly, "Well, I guess it's gettin' on 'bout suppertime."

His slow step down the sidewalk was the signal for the end of the day's talking. There were no farewells as the group dispersed. All the older men would be back on Monday afternoon to resume the conversation.

Conclusion

When *This Beats Working for a Living* first appeared, some professors who learned my identity—and who did not like the thought of anyone criticizing the academic world—said to me, "Well, if you feel that way about the business, why the hell don't you get out of it?" Or, as another said, "After reading the book, I concluded that you already had quit or else that you are going to do so very shortly."

Believe me, I have thought about quitting. But the mechanics of modern life in America demand that I have an income of some proportions—if not enough to support me in the style to which I would like to become accustomed, then at least to the genteel poverty to which my family has become accustomed. And if I had a third to half a million dollars stuck away in tax-free municipal bonds or even certificates of deposit, then I could walk away and call it quits forever.

And it is astonishing to me as I get around the country speaking or at academic conventions the number of professors who feel the same way. I have had several say, "This is not the business I got into. It has changed." Those of us who got into higher education twenty, fifteen, or even ten years ago had a sort of "Mr. Chips" image of the business. We would be kindly,

lovable professors teaching our classes and inspiring generations of students, meeting informally with the students one at a
time or in small gatherings to impart wisdom and guidance to
them, and doing some research which would result in benefits
to mankind.

Yet today we find ourselves pressured to attract yet more
students to the campus, teach them in large groups to keep cost
down (or even by television and never get to see them), fight for
grant money to bring prestige and recognition to our institution, get on academic programs for the same reason. In short,
the pressures of higher education today are much the same in
intensity of those in business and industry—but with salaries
that do not compare. As a friend of mine keeps saying, "If you
and I had just gone into industry or the law or medicine and
done the same amount of work, we'd be rich today."

This, of course, does not take into account all the recent
changes in higher education which make it even less attractive:
federal bureaucrats sniffing into all aspects of the business
(who said federal dollars would not bring federal strings?), the
new hardware approach to teaching that demands all of us have
the knowledge of a mechanical and an electrical engineer, the
push for unionization, and the scarcity of jobs.

Yet even with all of these things I have never seriously considered getting out of higher education, for despite the way I
have knocked at the profession in these two books by Professor
X I am a firm believer in the potential and the vital necessity of
our colleges and universities. Let me explain what I mean, and
the only way I know to do so is by a rather extended—and
serious—essay.

Throughout American history, people from other nations
have looked at our system of government and of society, a look
that has promoted a variety of comments: that we are fools
whom God has blessed; that we are conformists slavishly bound
to Coca Cola, juke boxes, rock music, and blue jeans; that ours
is a sick, decadent society; or that we are a hard-working people
who have been extremely generous with our wealth. We look at
ourselves and, depending on the eye of the beholder, see either

a permissive, hedonistic society bound for doom or else a healthy, viable society where the old verities of hard work, thrift, and morality are blessed. One of the distinguishing features of our society, in fact, is our mania for measuring everything from our opinions about television shows to the measure of confidence we have in our president. Perhaps no society in the history of the world has been so measured, analyzed, condemned, and praised. Certainly no other society in world history has been so imitated and envied.

Yet in our mad rush to know ourselves, one question has been repeated endlessly but never answered with finality, because there can be no final answer: what has kept democracy alive here? Other great democracies have risen only to fall. Why has ours endured? Another way of phrasing the same question is to ask, why has our revolution been a continuing one?—for American society has never settled into a rigid class structure. There has been no aristocratic class of enduring permanency. There are no permanently landed rich. There are no permanent political elites. Instead we have had, thanks to our constitution, a changing political elite that sees new congressmen every two years, new senators every six years, and a new president every four to eight years.

Thomas Jefferson, the third president, described our system as a "meritocracy," and he was right. The American political, economic, and social system has in the past been based on the practice of allowing men of merit to rise in industry, government, the arts, and all other forms of human endeavor. But always the question remained of how we permitted this to happen, how we held on to this. Other nations have had democratic constitutions but have evolved into societies based on class. Other nations have had capitalistic societies, but have had an enduring industrial and business clique that ruled from generation to generation.

What has made America unique in this respect?

Several observers of the American system have offered a theory that has gained wide acceptance: the frontier. Michel de Crèvecoeur, writting under the name J. Hector St. John, in

1782 published *Letters from an American Farmer,* in which he said that the newly arrived immigrant to the New World pushed out to the edge of the line of settlement; there he was forced to shed his European garb for the clothes of a frontiersman; there also he was forced to shed his European modes of thought and adopt those of the New World; there he dropped his old prejudices and attitudes to form new ones. In short, the frontier transformed him from a Frenchman or German or Englishman into an American. He concluded by saying:

> The American ought, therefore, to love his country much better than that wherein either he or his forefathers were born. Here the rewards of his industry follow with equal steps the progress of his labour, his labour is founded on the basis of nature, *self-interest;* can it want a stronger allurement. [Here no part of his] exuberant crops . . . [are claimed] by a despotic prince, a rich abbot, or a mighty lord. Here religion demands but little of him; a small voluntary salary to the minister, and gratitude to God; can he refuse these? The American is a new man, who acts upon new principles; he must therefore entertain new ideas, and form new opinions. From involuntary idleness, servile dependence, penury, and useless labor, he has passed to toils of a very different nature, rewarded by ample subsistence.—This is an American. . . .

One hundred and eleven years later Frederick Jackson Turner, a historian, focused his attention on the same question—and arrived at the same answer as Crèvecoeur: the frontier was responsible for promoting democracy and Americanism. In 1893 the young Turner gave an address before the American Historical Association entitled "The Significance of the Frontier in American History." In this he asserted that the frontier was *the* decisive factor in welding together an American nation and nationality distinct from other nations and nationalities, as well as in producing distinctly American traits. The frontier, to Turner, was a state of mind as well as the area of sparse settlement where "savagery met civilization." It was the area where the dominant traits were individualism, freedom, inquisitiveness, ingeniousness, materialism, strength, a laxness of business morals—and democracy.

On the frontier, according to Turner, most individuals were placed at a similar economic level, leading to a firm belief by these frontiersmen in political programs for the good of the common man—implying government programs for social amelioration, as well as government programs encouraging individualism, freedom of opportunity, and the acquisition of wealth. The frontier, moreover, was a "safety valve of abundant resources open to him who would take," meaning that the natural resources of the nation should be exploited. In line with this thesis, the frontiersmen wanted the public domain passed into private ownership as rapidly as possible so that it could be put to productive use.

All of this resulted in an American nationalism that favored lenient land legislation, internal improvements at government expense, a protective tariff, and a strong central government. Yet, paradoxically, it also meant a hearty dislike for authority, a belief in individual initiative, and the free-enterprise concept. This new man, this American, became noted for getting things done. He excelled in the production of tangibles, and thus had little time for philosophizing. In fact, America has produced only one school of philosophy—pragmatism.

And we are not known for introspection and contemplation, but for work! All the words used to describe a good frontiersman—independence, courage, self-reliance, initiative, individualism, industry—imply work. On the frontier the man who painted a picture or composed a symphonic piece had no one to view or listen to the result, but if he cultivated his fields he had food on the table during the winter. He could see tangible results from his labor, but not from philosophizing.

And this attitude about practicality and work was reflected in the folk heroes of the day. Back in Europe the folk tales had been concerned with princes and princesses, with vacant kingdoms and fairy godmothers. Here the folk tales dealt with Paul Bunyon, who could cut more timber than any other man; Pecos Bill, the cowboy; Casey Jones, the railroader; and Kemp

Morgan, the oil well driller. Note that all of these folk heroes were *workers*. Even our universities and colleges developed along different lines from those in Europe; ours trained students to work at specific tasks—as accountants, engineers, scientists—while those of Europe trained people (supposedly) to think. Only after the European graduated was he told to look for some practical application for his education. He might just as well have been taught to collect mustache cups or blue Amberola Edison records for all the practical value his education was to him.

Yet according to the census of 1890—and Frederick Jackson Turner noted the fact—the free land in the West was largely gone. No longer could young men seeking a new start or older men looking for a place to start over again find free or even inexpensive land in the West. And if it was the frontier of free or inexpensive land that had kept democracy alive during the early years of the republic, what replaced it (and here I think most of us would agree that democracy has flourished in the years since 1890)?

I submit that it was education, especially higher education, that has prevented class lines from becoming rigid during the 20th century. Especially do I believe it was the ease with which any determined person could acquire a higher education. The average poor youth desirous of advancing his economic status in life has found in this technological age that a college degree is the key that unlocks the door of opportunity. Anyone wanting to be an officer in the military service needs a bachelor's degree. Anyone wanting to work at the white collar level finds this type of employment easiest to get through a college placement service. Anyone wanting to enter the civil service at a level above GS 7, other than through political appointment, finds the civil service examination for these openings easier with college preparation.

Surveys by various organizations have proven these figures. For example, one survey showed that 94.3 percent of the presidents of major industrial firms are university graduates. Moreover, another survey found that approximately 90 percent of all self-made millionaires since World War II have been in the fields of electronics and real estate; given the sophistication of the electronics industry, most people therein find they need higher education. True, there are occasional individuals who make great fortunes and great contributions without benefit of college training, but the vast majority of America's youth find they need what the university has to offer.

(Here I want to add as an aside that it pleases me greatly to read about some self-made millionaire. So long as it is possible for Americans to cross class lines through hard work, intelligence, and, yes, even luck, then the republic is in no danger of developing a permanent aristocracy.)

Therefore I argue—and most vehemently—that it is in the interest of all concerned and patriotic Americans to see that educational opportunities are available to all. The combined cost of tuition, textbooks, fees, and living must never be allowed to rise above the pockets of those students who wish to work their way through college. If only the rich can afford to send their children to college, then we indeed will be approaching a rigid economic and social class structure in America.

Every time tuition costs rise, the hue and cry is raised for additional scholarship monies and loans to be made available to students. But we cannot and must not rely on federal programs to supply this money, else we will be allowing a set of federal bureaucrats to determine who the next elite will be. We must, in the interest of democracy and the American way of life (which has produced an abundance beyond anything known in the world), see that the choice of going to college be left at the individual level, not at some bureaucratic level. Anyone who has lived any lenth of time knows the danger of allowing the government to run almost any type of program. Nor should this be a decision left to college professors sitting on scholarship committees. Rather freedom dictates that it remain an individual decision—which it can be only so long as costs remain reasonable enough for any determined student to work his way through.

Our job, then, is two-fold. We must persuade (perhaps edu-

137

cate is a better word) our legislators to increase appropriations so that universities can operate without raising tuition. The costs of higher education cannot be paid solely by the students; rather, this is an investment in democracy that should be borne by the state and by interested individual donors. The long-range benefits of widely available higher education are such that we cannot afford to neglect it in the interest of short-range economies. To make the students pay all this cost will be a long-range disaster.

And, second, we must insist that our college and university instructors actually educate the students who come to them. Greatness as a nation will not come from repeating ideas hoary with age, reading lecture notes out-of-date before the last great war, and telling students that our system is bankrupt. In short, we must have true education take place in higher education, the kind that turns out people capable of solving problems, or working in industry and business, and of catering to our aesthetic needs.

What I am saying, for those of you who skipped this part, is that I believe higher education has value, that in fact it is the availability of higher education which has kept democracy viable in America, and that I am pleased to be a part of this—for it enabled me to rise up the economic ladder.

Therefore I am not getting out of the business. Instead, I am calling on those in it to try to better the system. I have written these two Professor X books, therefore, for two very noble motives: first, I wanted to use the vehicle of satire to make professors more aware of their obligations, even to work a little at their jobs (and if we do not, then it will be forced on us). And, second, I wanted to help the American economic system; I wanted to prove the words of Commodore Vanderbilt that "What's good for America is good for me," for if the book sells it will generate profits for the publisher, the printer, the bookseller, and the lumberjack, not to overlook the author.